UNFREE

SPEECH

UNFREE

THE THREAT TO GLOBAL DEMOCRACY

SPEECH

AND WHY WE MUST ACT, NOW

JOSHUA

WONG

With Jason Y. Ng

INTRODUCTION BY AI WEIWEI

PENGUIN BOOKS

WH
ALLEN

3 5 7 9 10 8 6 4 2

WH Allen, an imprint of Ebury Publishing,
20 Vauxhall Bridge Road,
London SW1V 2SA

WH Allen is part of the Penguin Random House group of companies
whose addresses can be found at global.penguinrandomhouse.com

First published by WH Allen in 2020

www.penguin.co.uk

A CIP catalogue record for this book is available from the British Library

ISBN 9780753554791

Printed and bound in Great Britain by Clays Ltd, Elcograf S.p.A.

Penguin Random House is committed to a sustainable future
for our business, our readers and our planet. This book is made from
Forest Stewardship Council® certified paper.

MIX
Paper from
responsible sources
FSC® C018179

*For those who have lost their freedom
fighting for Hong Kong*

Contents

ACT III: THE THREAT TO GLOBAL DEMOCRACY

Introduction: A New Generation of Rebel

前言: 新一代抗爭者

Joshua Wong represents a new generation of rebel. They were born into the globalised, post-internet era, raised in the late 1990s and early 2000s under a modern societal and knowledge structure that was relatively democratic and free. Their worldview is markedly different from that of the established capitalist culture fixated on profit above all else.

From the Umbrella Movement in 2014 to today's protests that have spurred on over a hundred days of resistance, we have seen the rise of a very special and brand-new rebel in Hong Kong. Joshua and his contemporaries are the vanguard of this phenomenon. They are rational and principled, clear as crystal in their objectives and as accurate as numbers. All they require and demand is a single value: freedom. They believe that through safeguarding the liberties of every citizen by demonstrating their rights in a highly visible way, we can achieve justice and democracy in any society.

This generation understands, lucidly, that freedom is not a given condition; rather, it is something to achieve through constant effort and struggle. These young people have borne a great responsibility, and many are now suffering because of it. Some have lost their promising young lives. But these activists can and will reach their goal, because we all know that freedom without hardship is not true freedom.

True freedom finds its value in hard work and determination. This is what Joshua's generation have come to realise through their own experiences. They are confronted with an authoritarian regime – an embodiment of centralised state power and the repression of human rights that we see in China and in other countries around the world. The scale of what this regime symbolises elevates the efforts of Joshua's generation to a heroism found in myths: the underdog locked in a struggle against powerful dark forces. I am confident that the citizens of Hong Kong, and those who march for their own rights and causes elsewhere, will overcome the massive establishment and will shape the world with the most powerful message: freedom, justice, and liberty for all.

Joshua's generation advocates for two of the most precious values created by humankind over thousands of years: social fairness and justice. These are the most important cornerstones of any civilisation. Throughout history, in pursuit of these principles humans have paid a great price, with too many deaths, misfortunes, betrayals and grave instances of opportunism.

Today we see that betrayal and opportunism everywhere in the so-called free world. In the West, it is ubiquitous. Joshua's generation is openly challenging all of these acts of duplicity, weakness and evasion in the name of defending humanity's core beliefs.

The young people of Hong Kong are realising a great social ideal in the spirit of sacrifice, similar to faith or religion. Together, their actions, their inherent understanding of the conflict and their awareness of the difficult realities they face are helping the whole world recognise what a real revolution is. This is what we have been waiting for, and I hope that the revolution, guided by Joshua and his generation, will be witnessed all over the world.

Ai Weiwei
18 October 2019

Foreword

推薦序

One of the immutable laws of history is that you cannot defeat an idea by locking up its proponents. That is not changed because of some alleged differences in the world's great civilisations – indeed some of the most important lessons about democracy, self-determination and civil disobedience have been taught by Asians, from Mahatma Gandhi to Kim Dae-jung.

Nor does it seem to me to speak to the long-term sustainable health and vitality of a community if its leaders cannot deal with dissent without trying to choke it off. You can censor the expression of free thought through curbing speeches on the internet, jailing journalists or even trying to stamp out jokes (under no circumstances allow yourself to mention any of the characters in *Winnie-the-Pooh* in Beijing, especially if you are holding a yellow umbrella!).

Nor, however mighty you may be, can you prevent people from thinking; moreover, sooner or later the good things they think drive out the bad things that authoritarians seek to impose.

The reason why the world beyond Hong Kong has viewed with admiration the courage, determination and eloquence of Joshua Wong and his colleagues is that what they seek is, on the whole, so reasonable and so obviously an effort to working with the grain of human aspiration as it was, is and will remain. Casuistical suggestions that the only way to deal with Joshua and his friends is to resort to the rule of law come ill from those who kept quiet and looked the other way when men were abducted from Hong Kong by the secret police of the Chinese Communist Party, with no care for the autonomy and law of Hong Kong. Perhaps what others saw never really happened.

Joshua and his colleagues know that I have never supported those who want a campaign for accountability, democracy, freedom of speech and assembly, autonomous universities and a vigorous and untrammelled civil society to be turned into pressure to achieve Hong Kong's independence. That is a dangerous blind alley. But reasonable people should ask themselves how and why this has happened.

How has the growing activity of China's United Front in Hong Kong – the attempt to throttle the promised autonomy of the community – increased the patriotism of a whole generation? Of course the very reverse of what was intended has resulted. What all that has done is not to make people feel less Chinese, but more proud of being *Hong Kong* Chinese. It's odd that the Chinese Communist Party has achieved something which the British colonial government never managed.

A short while ago, I had two encounters which worried me. The first was with a young Hong Kong woman in tears who asked me what could be done to prevent the erosion of freedom in the city she loved. The second was the remark of a senior banker (who had worked in Hong Kong for years) that, for the first time, he was starting to worry about Hong Kong's future.

I think that in many ways Joshua Wong and his friends are a sort of answer to both these worried lovers of Hong Kong. So long as their spirit is not snuffed out – and it won't be – I am sure that Hong Kong will survive as a symbol of the potential of humanity to create great things out of little. And I hope in the meantime that the world will watch closely to see how far China can be trusted to keep her word. Speaking for myself, and for most others, I trust Joshua of Hong Kong far more than the Communist apparatchiks of Beijing or their apologists in the city and elsewhere.

Chris Patten
Last Governor of Hong Kong
May 2018

Prologue

序幕

———

In August 2017, as the baking sun bore down on the streets of Hong Kong and university students were finishing up their summer jobs or returning from family trips, I was sentenced to six months in prison for my role in the Umbrella Movement that sent shock waves through the world and changed Hong Kong's history. I was immediately taken to Pik Uk Correctional Institution, a short walk from the school I used to attend. I was 20 years old.

The Department of Justice had won their appeal to increase my sentence from 80 hours of community service to a prison term – the first time anyone in Hong Kong was sentenced to jail for the charge of unlawful assembly. In doing so, the appeal had also made me one of the city's first political prisoners.

I had planned to keep a journal while I was in prison, both to make the time go by faster and to record the many conversations and events I was privy to within the prison walls. I thought that perhaps one day I would turn those notes into a book – and here it is.

This book comprises three acts. The first chronicles my coming of age, from a 14-year-old student campaign organiser to the founder of a political party and the face of a resistance movement against the ever-reaching long arm of Communist China in Hong Kong and beyond. It is a genesis story that lays bare a tumultuous decade of grassroots activism that lifted a population of 7 million out of political apathy into a heightened sense of social justice, capturing the imagination of the international community in the process.

In the second act, readers will find stories and anecdotes from my summer behind bars, captured in letters written every evening after I returned to my prison cell, as I sat on my hard bed and put pen to paper under dim light. I wanted to share my views on the state of the political movement in Hong Kong, the direction it should take, and how it is expected to shape our future. I also wanted to capture the essence of prison life, from my dialogues with prison staff to time spent with other inmates watching the news on television and trading stories of prisoner abuse. The experience brought me ever closer to other imprisoned activists like Martin

Luther King Jr and Liu Xiaobo – giants who inspired and guided me in spirit through the city's darkest hours and my own.

The book closes with an urgent call for all of us around the world to defend our democratic rights. Recent incidents, from the US National Basketball Association social media controversy to Apple's removal of a police-tracking app in Hong Kong, have shown that the erosion of freedoms that has plagued Hong Kong is spreading to the rest of the world. If multinationals, international governments and indeed ordinary citizens do not start paying attention to Hong Kong and treating our story as an early warning signal, it won't be long before everyone else feels the same invasion of civil liberties that Hong Kongers have endured and resisted every day on our streets for the past two decades.

Through *Unfree Speech* – my first book written for the international audience, I hope readers will get to know a young man in transition, both in mindset and in experience. But the book also reveals a city in transition, from a British colony to a special administrative region under Communist rule, from a concrete jungle of glass and steel to an urban battlefield of gas masks and umbrellas, from a pre-eminent financial hub to a shining bastion of freedom and defiance in the face of a global threat. These transitions have made me more committed than ever to the fight for a better Hong Kong – a cause that has defined my adolescence and continue to shape who I am.

Every day at Pik Uk Prison began with the same, exacting morning march: each inmate was expected to fall in line, march, halt, make a 90-degree turn, look up at the guards and announce their presence one after the other. Every day I heard myself shouting those same words at the top of my lungs: 'Good morning, Sir! I, Joshua Wong, prison number 4030XX, have been convicted of unlawful assembly. Thank you, SIR!'

I am Joshua Wong. My prison number was 4030XX. And this is my story.

ACT I

GENESIS

'Let no man despise thy youth; but be thou an example of the believers, in word, in conversation, in charity, in spirit, in faith, in purity.'

– 1 Timothy 4:12

To the Promised Land: The Rise of the New Hong Konger

到應許之地：新香港人的崛起

I was born in 1996, the Year of the Fire Rat, nine months before Hong Kong reverted to Chinese rule.

According to the Chinese Zodiac, which runs on a 60-year cycle, the fire rat is adventurous, rebellious and garrulous. Although as a Christian I believe in neither Western nor Eastern astrology, these personality predictions are fairly spot on – especially the part about me being a compulsive talker.

'When Joshua was still a baby, even with a bottle in his mouth he would make all sorts of sounds like he was giving a speech on stage.' This is the way my mum still introduces me to new church people. I don't have the faintest memory of what I did as a baby, but her description is entirely believable and I take her word for it.

When I was seven years old I was diagnosed with dyslexia, a writing and reading disorder. My parents had noticed the signs early on when I had trouble with even basic Chinese characters. Simple words that preschoolers learned in a matter of days, like 'large' (大) and 'very' (太), looked indistinguishable to me. I would make the same mistakes in homework assignments and exams well into my teens.

But my speech was unaffected by my learning disability. By speaking confidently I was able to make up for my weaknesses. The microphone loved me and I loved it even more. As a child I would tell jokes in church groups and ask questions that even the bigger kids wouldn't dare ask. I would bombard the pastor and church elders with queries like 'If God is so full of mercy and kindness, why does He let poor people suffer in caged homes in Hong Kong?' and 'We make donations to the church every month, where does the money go?'

When my parents took me on trips to Japan and Taiwan I would grab the tour guide's megaphone and share factoids I'd found on the internet about places to see and things to do, moving from topic to topic like it was the most natural thing in the world. The audience would cheer their approval.

My motormouth and innate inquisitiveness earned me praise and chuckles wherever I went. Thanks to my small stature and chubby cheeks, what might otherwise have been considered annoying or overbearing was forgiven as 'cute', 'quirky' or 'precocious'. While there were teachers and parents who wished this little know-it-all would shut up occasionally, they were usually in the minority and I was doted on in school and at church. 'Your boy is special. He'll make a great lawyer one day!' the churchgoers would tell my father.

In the West, people may see an aspiring politician or rights activist in an outspoken child, but in Hong Kong – one of the world's most capitalistic regions – neither of these career choices would be wished upon even your worst enemy. A lucrative career in law, medicine or finance is the epitome of success in every parent's eyes. But mine aren't like that and they didn't raise me that way.

My parents are both devout Christians. My father was an IT professional before he took early retirement to focus on church affairs and community work. My mother works at a local community centre that provides family counselling. They married in 1989, just weeks after the Chinese government sent in the tanks to crush student demonstrators on Tiananmen Square. My mum and dad agreed to cancel their wedding celebrations and sent out handwritten notes to friends and relatives with a simple message: 'Our nation is in crisis, the newlyweds shall not stand on ceremony.' In a culture where an expensive wedding banquet is as much a rite of passage as the act of getting married itself, their decision was both bold and noble.

My Chinese name, Chi-fung, was inspired by the Bible. The characters 之鋒 mean 'something sharp', a reference to Psalm 45:5, which instructs, 'Send your sharp arrows through enemy hearts and make all nations fall at your feet.' My parents didn't want me to pierce anyone's heart, but they did want me to speak the truth and wield it like a sword to cut through lies and injustice.

Other than my unusual loquaciousness, I was a pretty typical child. My best friend in primary school was Joseph. He was taller than me, better looking, and got better marks. He could easily have hung out with the popular kids, but we bonded over our common tendency to prattle on and on, chatting during class despite sitting seven seats apart. In Primary Two (ages 6–7) our teacher Mr Szeto was so fed up with our non-stop talking that he petitioned the head to put us in different classes in the following year groups. But that didn't work.

Joseph and I were inseparable. We would meet up at each other's flats after school to play video games and trade manga comic books. The first movie I ever watched in a cinema was *Batman: The Dark Knight*, a Hollywood blockbuster set partially in Hong Kong – and I watched it with Joseph.

We had something else in common. My class was the first to be born after the Handover. We are the generation that entered this world during the most important political event in Hong Kong's history. On 1 July 1997, after 156 years of British rule, Hong Kong shed its colonial past and returned to Communist China. The sovereignty transfer was meant to be a cause for celebration – a reunification between mother and child and an opportunity for the local business elite to tap the still emerging mainland market – except that for most ordinary Hong Kongers it wasn't. Many of our relatives and friends had left Hong Kong years before that fateful date out of fear of Communist rule. By the time I was born nearly half a million citizens had emigrated to countries like the US, the UK, Canada, Australia and New Zealand. To them, communism was synonymous with the political turmoil that resulted from the Great Leap Forward – a failed economic campaign between 1958 and 1962 to industrialise China that caused the death of an estimated 30 million peasants from mass starvation – and the Cultural Revolution – a sociopolitical movement between 1966 and 1976 led by Chairman Mao Zedong to purge capitalistic tendencies and political rivals. Communism was the reason why they and their parents had fled to Hong Kong in the first place; the idea of being handed back to the 'thieves and murderers' – to use my grandmother's words – from whom they had escaped was terrifying and inconceivable.

But it was all hearsay as far as I was concerned. To someone who grew up knowing only Chinese rule, those accounts were nothing more than tales and urban legends. The only flag I had seen flying in public places and outside government buildings was the Five-starred Red Chinese flag. Other than the London-style double-decker buses and English-sounding street names like Hennessy, Harcourt and Connaught, I don't have any memory of colonial Hong Kong or feel any attachment to British rule. Even though many local schools like the one I attended continue to teach in English, students are taught to take pride in the many economic achievements of modern China, not least the way the Chinese Communist Party had lifted hundreds of millions of people out of abject poverty. At school we learned that the Basic Law, Hong Kong's mini-constitution and a heavily negotiated document that China and Britain laboured over before the Handover, begins with the declaration that 'The Hong Kong Special Administrative Region is an inalienable part of the People's Republic of China'. China is our motherland and, like a benevolent parent, she will always have our best interests in mind under the so-called 'one country, two systems' framework.

The principle was memorialised in the Sino-British Joint Declaration, an international treaty signed by Britain and China in 1984. 'One country, two systems' was the brainchild of the then paramount leader Deng Xiaoping, who needed a solution to stem the exodus of talent and wealth from Hong Kong during the Handover talks. Deng wanted to reassure fleeing citizens that the city would be reunited with mainland China without losing its distinct economic and political systems. He famously promised the city that 'horses will still run, and dancers will still dance' under Chinese rule.

Deng's strategy worked. 'One country, two systems' helped Hong Kong transition smoothly from a Crown colony to a special administrative region. For most people, the Handover turned out to be much ado about nothing. Shortly after the clock struck midnight on 30 June 1997, 7 million Hong Kongers with their eyes glued to the television screen watched Chris Patten, the last colonial Governor, walk out of the Governor's House for the last time. As Patten boarded the Royal Yacht *Britannia*, accompanied by Prince Charles, everyone heaved a sigh of relief that, despite the dramatic pomp and circumstance, almost nothing had changed in Hong Kong. Many people thought that those who had fled the city out of fear had overreacted and underestimated China's goodwill.

My first encounter with 'one country, two systems' was more visceral than international treaties and constitutional frameworks. When I was five, my parents took me on a short holiday to Guangzhou, the capital city of Guangdong Province, of which Hong Kong is also a part. It was 2001, the same year that China joined the World Trade Organization and began its economic miracle.

Back then, Guangzhou was still a backwater compared with Hong Kong. Internet connection was patchy and many websites were blocked. Even though people in Guangzhou spoke Cantonese like we do, they behaved differently – in Hong Kong we never squat or spit in the streets; we always queue up and wait our turn to speak to sales or service people. Not so in China.

What's more, cars drove on the other side of the road and shoppers paid with tiny tattered notes called *renminbi*. Signage and menus were in simplified Chinese characters that looked familiar but not quite the same as the traditional ones we used in Hong Kong. Even Coca-Cola tasted different because the water they used had a funny aftertaste. 'I prefer the way things are in Hong Kong,' I remember telling myself.

From my parents' generation to mine, children in Hong Kong have grown up with anime from Japan. By far the most advanced economy in Asia, Japan has long been considered by Hong Kongers a trend-setting culture and exporter of all things cool. I've been a diehard fanboy of a sci-fi series called *Gundam,* Japan's answer to the Marvel and DC franchises. Many of my favourites – such as *Mobile Suit Gundam OO, Gundam Seed* and *Iron-Blooded Orphans* – share a common thread: they each tell the story of a young orphan who struggles to find their place in the world as they move from one foster family to the next.

The recurring theme of foster children in my Saturday morning cartoons makes me think about my own city. In many ways, Hong Kong is just like a foster child who was raised by a white family and, without his consent, returned to his Chinese biological parents. Mother and son have very little in common, from language and customs to the way they view their government. The more the child is forced to show affection and gratitude toward his long-lost mother, the more he resists. He feels lost, abandoned and alone. 'One country, two systems' may have navigated the former colony through its smooth transition to Chinese rule in 1997, but it does little to ease its deepening identity crisis. Hong

Kong is a city that isn't British and doesn't want to be Chinese, and its need to assert a distinct identity grows by the year.

This about sums up the state of mind of my generation – the first to grow up after the end of British rule, but before Chinese rule had taken hold. The ambivalence my generation feels towards our purported motherland motivates us to search for ways to fill the emotional void. We are struggling to carve our place in the world and develop an identity in our own image. More and more we look to our pop culture, language, food and unique way of life as the foundations of that self-image. Efforts to preserve quaint neighbourhoods, support local products and protect Cantonese from its replacement by Mandarin are gradually evolving into a youth crusade.

When I was ten years old, the biggest news story in Hong Kong was about massive protests to save two beloved and historically important ferry piers – the Star Ferry Pier and the Queen's Pier – from demolition. The campaigns were about more than a pushback against cold-hearted urban redevelopment and gentrification: they were about defending our fledgling identity. Those spurts of resistance and anger were only the tip of the iceberg. The rise of the new Hong Konger had only just begun.

*

But my political coming of age was put on hold when I turned twelve. As soon as I began my last year of primary, the only thing that mattered to me and my classmates was getting admitted to a decent secondary school. We have a saying in Hong Kong: 'high school is destiny'; it isn't an overstatement. The local education system is cut-throat and the school we attend has the power to determine our future: which university we get into, which course we choose, what kind of job we get when we graduate, how much money we make, who we can date and marry and, ultimately, the level of respect we will be able to command from society. That's why so-called 'helicopter parents' go to great lengths to design elaborate 'portfolios' for their children to make them more marketable to schools. Mastery of multiple musical instruments and exotic foreign languages are the rule rather than the exception.

I wasn't optimistic. Without a killer CV and with a report card hamstrung by dyslexia I knew it would be a struggle. But I wasn't going to give up. If Moses could spend 40 years wandering in the desert before Joshua finished the job and led his people to the Promised Land, what was a bit of hard work for this fire rat?

There's a common Chinese saying: 'diligence can make up for all shortcomings'. That year, I put away my video games and manga and put in over 20 hours of private tutoring every week. I worked especially hard on my weakest subjects – Chinese and English – which tended to bring down my grades. As a result of my hard work, I managed to score 0.1 points above the minimum grade point average I'd needed to get me on my primary school's 'recommended students' list. Thanks to my outspoken requests, both the head and my form teacher agreed to write reference letters touting not academic prowess per se, but rather my 'potential to excel'.

At the final round interview for secondary school, the admissions officer asked me, 'If one of your friends told you he had been bullied, what would you do, Joshua?' Without a thought, I shot back an answer as if I had been asked the same question a hundred times: 'I would take my friend to church and let God guide him. I might even do the same for the bullies. God has a plan for everyone.' The officer smiled and I smiled back. The next thing I knew, I got a letter informing me that I'd been admitted to United Christian College after someone else had forfeited his offer. The school was my first choice.

The Great Leap Forward: Scholarism and National Education

大躍進：學民思潮與國民教育

Secondary school was refreshing. Instead of being treated like children, as we had been for six years in primary school, we were now young adults, given the latitude to express our opinions in class and run our own activities after school. What's more, the school curriculum was less about rote learning and memorisation and focused more on analysis and critical thinking, which meant my dyslexia was not as big a disadvantage as it used to be.

I loved taking pictures and videos, so I went everywhere with my handheld camera, capturing moments in school, big and small. I would upload my photos to my Facebook page and meticulously organise them into albums. I also started my own blog to document school events with funny commentaries. It quickly gained traction and soon had thousands of followers, many of whom were parents eager to find out what their children were up to during the week. Despite being a newcomer at United Christian College, I quickly made a name for myself as the school journalist, filmmaker and gossip columnist. But among my friends I was mostly known as a *dokuo*, the Japanese term for a young man with no girlfriend who delights in being left alone with their video games and gadgets.

Girlfriendless or not, I saw myself more like the child in Hans Christian Andersen's 'The Emperor's New Clothes' who, when none of the townsfolk would say what was on their minds, took it upon himself to point out the elephant in the room – and there were so many elephants in the local education system. One time my Chinese teacher, who had lost patience with my constant talking in class, ordered me to be quiet and stand in the corner. As I got up from my seat I looked him in the eye and said, 'This is no way to teach a child. Do you honestly think I'll become a better student by facing the wall?' My question left the teacher speechless and the rest of the class stunned.

My penchant for challenging the authorities soon took a new turn as I combined my outspokenness with the power of social media.

I had always enjoyed good food and considered my palate as sharp as my tongue. In Secondary Two (ages 13–14), after suffering a whole year of subpar canteen food at UCC, I decided to take matters into my own hands. I set up a Facebook page and online petition and invited all my classmates to voice their grievances over the school catering's bland, oily and overpriced lunch boxes. The campaign went viral and more than 10 per cent of the school signed the petition.

Because of its popularity, the unprecedented campaign, titled 'How much longer should we tolerate bad food at UCC?', immediately caught the attention of the school authorities. A few days later I was called into the principal's office with my parents. 'Joshua is a nice boy,' Principal To said to my parents, before narrowing his eyes, 'but what he did wasn't . . . well . . . ideal. He instigated other students and put us in a difficult position. Worse than that, he named our school in a public petition without our approval.' 'But with all due respect, our boy hasn't done anything wrong,' my father said, jumping to my defence, before my mother, ever the peacemaker, offered a sensible assessment with which even Principal To had to agree. 'Look, the Facebook page is already out there,' she said. 'If you make Joshua take it down, the repercussions will be much worse. I think we should just let it be.' Thanks to my parents, I walked out of the head's office unscathed; no suspension or any form of disciplinary action.

But that was the first and last time I organised a social media campaign at school. I decided to stop, not for fear of getting into trouble again, but because I realised there were bigger fish to fry. Why bother with petty issues in high school when there were far greater injustices playing out every day and right under our noses? I decided to set my sights much higher and focus on bigger, more pressing things.

A few weeks before the canteen petition, I'd had an epiphany. It happened during a regular community visit on an ordinary Saturday afternoon. My father is a devout Christian and spends much of his spare time volunteering. I used to accompany him on his visits to the elderly, to underprivileged families and children with special needs.

On this particular Saturday, we went to a senior citizens' home that we had visited a year before. A few dozen octogenarians had already taken their seats in a big circle in the day room, expecting us. I recognised the same peeling pastel walls and tattered furniture from a year ago; I saw the same faces staring back at me; the home was every bit as short-staffed, the amenities as dated and the residents as lonely and destitute as they were when my father and I left them last time we came. My eyes welled up despite myself, but deep down I was more angry than sad.

I asked my dad, 'What's the point of these visits? What's the point if nothing ever changes?' He answered with a pat on my shoulder. 'We cheered them up for a couple of hours, didn't we? Let's keep them in our prayers. That's the best we or the church can do.'

As much as I respected my father, I couldn't disagree with him more. There was much more we could do for these people, only we hadn't tried hard enough. It wasn't fair that my family could live in a middle-class neighbourhood, attend a fancy mega-church and go on overseas holidays while nearly a fifth of the local population struggled below the poverty line, with barely enough to eat and no decent home to live in.

In school we learned that Hong Kong has one of the world's highest Gini coefficients, a measure of income inequality. That's why every day we see old people picking through rubbish bins and pushing heavy carts of recycled paper up hills to sell them on for a pittance; it's such a common sight that we no longer even notice them. All this is allowed to continue because too many people think like middle-class churchgoers: let's pray and pretend we've done enough.

I was convinced that God had put me on this world for a reason: He wanted me to do more than just praise His name and study the Bible. He wanted me to take action. My father once taught me the acronym WWJD, which stands for 'What would Jesus do?' I didn't think Jesus would walk out of that senior citizens' home with a self-congratulatory pat on the shoulder. If He did I would call Him a hypocrite, just like the boy who calls out the naked emperor.

After this episode I began to feel restless. I'd realised that there is often a gulf between good intentions and actions, but I didn't know what, in practical terms, I might actually do for the people in that home, or anyone else for that matter. Crucially, this turning point in my adolescence happened not long before I met my partner-in-crime at UCC.

Justin was another *dokuo* in my class and we shared the same passions for video games, anime and getting up to mischief in school. During the summer holiday after Primary Two, two of our favourite teachers announced their plan to marry. Justin and I decided to create a sketch in their honour. He played the groom and we enlisted a bunch of other classmates to play the bride and her well-wishing relatives. I was the filmmaker who recorded the mock wedding. To up the emotional impact I even added a soundtrack. When the newlyweds finally saw the video on YouTube they were moved to tears.

Incidents like this spread through the school like wildfire and, despite causing trouble from time to time, they made us our teachers' favourites. They also made Justin and me best friends.

But Justin provided much more than companionship. He had been a politics junkie long before we met. 'This stuff is what really matters,' he would say to me matter-of-factly while swiping through news feeds about local elections and government bills on his iPhone.

Over time, some of his hot-bloodedness began to rub off on me. We would visit local bookstores together and spend hours in the politics section. We would trade books with one another, instantly doubling the number of titles at our disposal.

I spent the summer of 2009, when I was 12 years old, reading up on local politics and discussing what I learnt with Justin. 'This is insane!' I remember shouting after I had read about Hong Kong's bizarre electoral system and how it had been designed to help government stonewall the opposition. 'Our government is so messed up. Why is it that no one ever talks about this?' I exclaimed in exasperation.

Justin rolled his eyes as if to say, 'I'm glad you've finally caught up. Welcome to Hong Kong!'

Our political system is truly one of a kind. It is the product of numerous painful – some say callous – concessions made by Britain during the Handover negotiations with China that resulted in the Basic Law.

The Basic Law prescribes three branches of government – the executive, legislature and judiciary. Under the system, ordinary citizens have no say in choosing the chief executive, the highest office in Hong Kong and the head of the executive branch, a position akin to the mayor of London or New York. Instead, he or she is selected by a small committee stacked with Communist Party loyalists, business tycoons and special interest groups, most of whom take cues from central government in Beijing before they cast their votes. The result is a head of government who is unaccountable to the people and who answers only to the bosses up north who have put them in office.

Our legislature isn't any better than the executive branch. The Legislative Council, or LegCo, is a 70-member parliament divided into two 35-member chambers: geographical constituencies (GCs) and functional constituencies (FCs, drawn from the business and professional sectors). Whereas the GCs are all elected by nearly 4 million registered voters, the FCs are far from democratically elected. Nearly all of the functional lawmakers are hand-picked by a small circle of voters within their own trade or special interest groups. For instance, the real estate functional seat is selected by a few hundred industry practitioners and construction companies, just as the legal and accountancy seats are selected only by licensed lawyers and accountants. Together, they constitute a powerful bloc of lawmakers who vote in lockstep with each other and at the bidding of the government. In other words, the FCs give the executive branch near-complete control over LegCo.

I learned all of this from my summer reading – and from many late night heart-to-hearts with Justin over video games and bubble tea. I felt angry and frustrated that such a blatantly unjust system had been allowed to fly under the radar for so long. I also came to realise that everything that's wrong with Hong Kong – from old-age poverty to skyrocketing property prices and the wanton destruction of historic buildings to make way for pork-barrel redevelopment projects – was attributable to a single culprit: our unaccountable government and the lopsided electoral system that created and facilitates it.

It didn't take me long to turn my political awakening into action. The following winter, in January 2010, a number of pro-democracy lawmakers resigned from office at the same time, triggering simultaneous by-elections to fill their seats. The idea was to turn the by-elections into a referendum on electoral reform and put pressure on the government to abolish the hated functional constituencies.

Ahead of the election, I composed a long Facebook post targeted at both students and their parents – especially the parents since they were old enough to vote. I spent hours drafting summaries and bullet points, condensing into plain language the convoluted political process so that any reader could understand what the referendum was about. I made a case for why Hong Kongers needed to work together to get rid of FCs once and for all. The post received over a thousand likes, which surprised me because no one knew who I was at the time and the subject matter itself wasn't the most enticing.

In the end, the government ignored the results of the by-elections and passed a disappointing electoral reform bill with only minor tweaks to the existing system. It fell far short of abolishing the FCs. Still, for a 13-year-old it was an important lesson in political activism: you can try as hard as you want, but until you force them to pay attention, those in power won't listen to you.

The real test would come after I celebrated my 14th birthday. In October 2010, the then Chief Executive Donald Tsang issued his last policy address before the end of his second term in office. According to the address, the government would introduce a school curriculum which introduced a new and mandatory subject called 'moral and national education'. This new subject had several objectives:

1.   development of moral qualities;
2.   development of a positive and optimistic attitude;
3.   self-recognition;
4.   judging in a caring and reasonable manner;
5.   recognition of identity.

Anodyne as these points sound, at the heart of the vagaries was a more sinister aim: to shape the first generation of Hong Kongers into the Chinese mould and teach us to accept and adopt Communist Party principles – without us, or our parents, even noticing. In Hong Kong, anything with the word 'national' in it arouses suspicion. The name 'national education' raises the spectre of Communist propaganda and brainwashing, the very kind that students in mainland China have been subject to – and have continued to suffer – for decades. If nothing was done about it, this new curriculum would be implemented in all primary schools in Hong Kong by 2012 and all secondary schools by 2013. A four-month public consultation would supposedly commence in 2011, but I knew that in reality, this 'consultation' would not result in any changes in the curriculum at all.

National education hit very close to home for me. It was the first government policy that deliberately targeted and directly impacted my classmates and me. I was a key stakeholder – a term we had just learned in liberal studies class at UCC. And if the people who had the most to lose didn't speak up, who else would?

Sure enough, during the four-month consultation period the pro-democracy lawmakers and even the teachers' union expressed only mild annoyance, responding to the Education Bureau with verbal disapproval and wagging fingers. 'These adults have all been out of school for two or three decades,' I said to Justin, 'why should they care about what goes on inside the classroom? But we need to care and we need to protect our education before it's too late.'

Justin's parents had a different plan for him. Mindful of his future, they were sending him abroad to finish his schooling. In a year's time he would leave Hong Kong and I would part with my best friend and my political muse.

Justin and I continued to hang out right up until he left for America, but deep down I knew that if I wanted to fight the Dark Force, I needed to recruit some new Jedis.

I zeroed in on Ivan Lam, a Secondary Four (ages 15–16) student at UCC. I'd befriended a number of like-minded students at street rallies and exchanged contact details – Ivan was one of them. Like Justin, Ivan had been politically active from a young age. The 16-year-old was also known for his artistic talent, having won many design competitions at UCC and beyond. I began to follow him to various anti-government protests and demonstrations, including the annual 1 July protest march that marks the anniversary of the Handover, and 4 June Tiananmen Square Massacre candlelight vigil, the two biggest events in Hong Kong's civil society calendar, both of which draw thousands of citizens onto the streets. Back then, not that many students would attend political gatherings so it was easy for us to spot each other, especially if we were wearing our school uniforms. The circle of friends we made at those rallies would later become the first members of our anti-national education campaign and provide the critical mass for its early events.

In May 2011, Ivan and I launched a Facebook page and named our group Scholarism, 'scholar' because we were a student group and 'ism' to signal a new way of thinking (and to give the name more gravitas).

Over the next few months we made banners, printed flyers, set up street stalls, staged small-scale sit-ins and recruited more student volunteers to do the same. Ivan was responsible for all of our campaign artwork; the use of snappy graphics and punchy sound bites was critical in spreading the word online. By May 2012, on Scholarism's one-year anniversary, our following had grown from a close-knit group of friends to 10,000 people. Among our members was Agnes Chow, who was the same age as me. Eloquent, strong-willed and linguistically gifted, she would become one of Scholarism's core members and its sole female spokesperson.

Founding Scholarism was a natural extension of what I had already been doing in the preceding year. It was the canteen petition all over again; except this time, it involved many more stakeholders and targeted an entire generation of young people. In fact, the idea of running our own youth activist group felt so natural that I didn't even discuss it with my parents before we launched it.

In the months following the creation of Scholarism, I spent nearly every day giving soapbox speeches on street corners and sitting for press interviews. I became a regular feature in the local media after one of my impromptu interviews went viral and was viewed 150,000 times within two weeks. My mum started saving newspaper clippings about me and recording the radio shows I appeared on. 'This is part of our history,' she would say. 'You are making history.'

But it wasn't all glamour and fame. For nearly 18 months I lived the life of Peter Parker. Like Spider-Man's alter ego, I went to class during the day and rushed out to fight evil after school. I would take the bus to the government headquarters in Admiralty – our equivalent of the Houses of Parliament or Capitol Hill – to meet with civil society leaders and pro-democracy lawmakers and discuss what could be done to stop the implementation of national education. While my peers sang karaoke and went to the movies, I was strategising Scholarism's next moves while coordinating mass protests with adults many years older than me. With donated funds we rented a tiny office in an industrial building and set up a campaign HQ there. I would miss important school assignments and even exams and, after a disastrous semester, fall to the bottom of the class. Fortunately, UCC was supportive of my efforts and gave me a pass. One time my maths teacher pulled me aside and said, 'I have a teenage girl who's about your age. I want to thank you for doing this for her.'

In July 2012, our anti-national education campaign intensified. Chun-ying (or C.Y.) Leung, a self-made millionaire widely rumoured to be an underground Chinese Communist Party member, took office to succeed Donald Tsang as chief executive. Soon after Leung was sworn in, a teaching manual published by a government-funded think tank was distributed to primary and secondary schools citywide. The manual praised the Chinese Communist Party as an 'advanced and selfless regime' and criticised Western democracy by arguing that 'toxic bipartisan politics' in the United States had led to the 'suffering of its people'. It confirmed all our suspicions and fears about Communist propaganda.

This bombshell publication set civil society ablaze. Within days a new alliance was formed comprising a dozen organisations, including Scholarism, the Hong Kong Federation of Students (HKFS) and Civil Human Rights Front (CHRF), the most prominent civil liberty group in the city. On 29 July I led the alliance in a massive street rally that attracted nearly 100,000 participants, most of them parents and students.

Despite the massive turnout, Leung's government, as I had expected, remained intransigent. Though Leung claimed that he was open to a dialogue with concerned groups, he reiterated that the curriculum would go ahead as planned. Heartbroken and enraged, Ivan took to the stage in Admiralty that night. Fighting back tears, he said, 'We don't need dialogue. We haven't come this far to make deals with politicians!' Within hours of his speech, another 700 student volunteers joined Scholarism.

By mid-August, more than 15 months since we began our campaign, there was a real sense of urgency within Scholarism. The new school year would be starting in a month's time and so would the new curriculum if we didn't stop it in time. 'Protests alone aren't enough,' I said to Ivan. 'We need to shift things up a gear.'

In the following weeks, Scholarism members fanned out across the city, stepping up their protests outside school entrances and launching a street petition campaign. Within a week we had collected 120,000 signatures from concerned students.

Supporters of all ages came by our street stalls to drop off pizzas, sushi, baked goods and drinks to keep us going.

With only days left before students were due to return to school, Ivan and I knew we had reached a now-or-never moment. On 31 August we called on students to head to Admiralty and occupy the front yard of the government headquarters. We baptised the open space with a new, symbolic – and catchy – name: 'Civic Square'.

On the same day, Ivan and two other Scholarism members began a hunger strike: the first of its kind by secondary school students in the city's history. The aim was to build public sympathy and attract more press coverage for our campaign. I wanted to go on hunger strike too, but Ivan said I should save my energy to do what I did best: speak to the press.

On 3 September, 72 hours after it began, our medical team ordered the three to end the strike as their blood sugar levels had become dangerously low. Ivan's lips had turned paper white and he was groggy and could barely sit up. Still, not a single government official bothered to visit them. In a PR stunt, C.Y. Leung showed up at Civic Square to shake hands with the demonstrators, without even checking on the hunger strikers.

By the end of the week, the anti-national education campaign had reached fever pitch. On Friday 7 September we called on parents and children to join us in a mass protest outside the government headquarters dressed in black, the colour of mourning. Thanks to our hunger strike and media blitz, over 120,000 black-clothed citizens descended on Admiralty after they finished work and school to show solidarity with the Scholarism demonstrators. It was the largest assembly without prior police approval in Hong Kong's history and the highest turnout ever for a rally organised by secondary school students. The crowds were so huge that protesters spilled over onto Harcourt Road, a major highway running through the city's financial district.

That night I gave the biggest speech I'd ever given. Everything I had learned from my parents, the church elders, my teachers and Justin culminated in that one moment. Even though I was exhausted from weeks of sleeping in a tent and giving interviews, I didn't want to let down all the people who believed in me and counted on me. I had to give it everything I had.

'This is the ninth straight day of our Civic Square sit-in,' I said in a hoarse voice as soon as I was handed the microphone — which I thought of as my weapon of choice, like Thor's hammer or Captain

America's vibranium shield. I was still only 15, after all. 'We've made history and shown Hong Kong and Beijing the power of the people. Tonight we have one message and one message only: C.Y. Leung, withdraw the brainwashing curriculum!'

The crowd cheered and I went from a shout to a roar: 'We've had enough of this government. Hong Kongers will prevail!'

On the following day, C.Y. Leung held a press conference announcing his decision to suspend the curriculum. We watched the announcement at the Teachers' Union conference room, which had been Scholarism's second home for the last 18 months. In front of the flickering television screen parents cried, students cheered, and activists were locked in a tight embrace.

I turned to Ivan and said, 'We've won!'

Where Are the Adults?
The Umbrella Movement

成年人在哪裡？雨傘運動

The anti-national education campaign catapulted us to political stardom. The members of Scholarism had gone from a group of young anti-government rebels to household names – and now history makers. Never before had a group of secondary school students led a political movement of such scale and with such success. Back at UCC, teachers came up to me and Ivan to shake our hands. Everyone at church gave me their congratulations. I didn't feel I deserved such praise and attention because I knew I didn't do it by myself – no one could. To every 'great job' and 'well done' I replied: 'The victory belongs to all of us. All I did was speak the truth.'

But I also understood the euphoria and excitement all around me. Political victories, like the mysterious tanhua flower that only blooms once in a blue moon, are rare for Hong Kongers. The last time a mass protest in Hong Kong had yielded tangible results was almost a decade before, in 2003, when under the disastrous leadership of the city's first Chief Executive Tung Chee-hwa the government was forced to scrap a controversial National Security Bill after half a million citizens took to the streets to demand its retraction. The hard-fought victory buoyed our spirits and strengthened our collective identity.

The axing of national education had the same effect on the city nine years later. It gave every freedom-loving citizen a shot in the arm and reminded them that they didn't need to roll over and play dead in the face of bad government policies. Real change could happen if we worked together.

But, euphoric as we felt, we knew better than to rest on our laurels. Hong Kong remained a city of freedom without democracy – citizens had the right to kick and scream but they still couldn't choose their government. As long as our political system stayed the same it was only a matter of time before another dangerous government initiative would erupt. And next time we might not be able to hold our ground. We had to set our sights on the ultimate goal of bringing universal suffrage to Hong Kong. Every time someone congratulated me on the national education win, I would respond in the same way: we might have won a battle, but the war is far from over. I wasn't being humble, it was the hard truth.

Hong Kongers are pragmatic. Few bother with political drivel like electoral reform that may or may not happen, much less benefit them in the short run. It is often said that there are two types of people in the city – those who don't care about politics and those who do but choose to do nothing about it. But where the adults have failed, young people will take up the mantle. If the national education campaign taught us one thing, it was that students have a say in adult issues. Politics is no longer an exclusive sport for grey-haired politicians and lifelong bureaucrats.

In 2012, if I had asked anyone on the streets what universal suffrage meant, very few people would have given me a straight answer. Fewer still would have told me that Beijing had promised the city the right to elect its own chief executive and the entire LegCo in a few years' time. Unbeknown to most Hong Kongers, there existed a largely forgotten political promise, an axis around which a full-scale popular uprising would soon turn.

To understand how this political promise came about, we have to go back to the early years of the Hong Kong Special Administrative Region of the People's Republic of China.

The first decade after the Handover was nothing short of catastrophic. Even though the transition to Chinese rule in 1997 had been smooth, the newly minted special administrative region began to crack under the weight of a regional debt crisis, a deadly epidemic and an incompetent government.

I was just a baby when a crippling financial crisis hit East and Southeast Asia in 1997. It took years for the region to recover and Hong Kong had barely got back on its feet when the 2002–3 SARS (a viral respiratory disease) outbreak killed nearly 300 people and decimated the local economy. I remember my parents taking me to a neighbourhood restaurant for dim sum that summer only to find the normally jam-packed dining hall completely deserted. It was like being in a post-apocalypse sci-fi movie.

And things got worse. Tung Chee-hwa's misguided housing policy led to the burst of the property bubble and the foreclosure of thousands of homes, sending the suicide rate to a record high. Then a controversial National Security Bill, which was required under the Basic Law but had never been enacted, proposed long jail terms for

sedition, secession or treason and gave the government greater rights to arrest citizens and ban
political organisations that are deemed a threat to
national security. It was the straw that broke the
camel's back – 500,000 angry citizens marched
down Hennessy Road in the largest ever 1 July rally
to demand government accountability and political
reform.

I was too young to march at the time, but my
parents were there. I asked my mum why she had
gone and she replied, 'Once the bill is passed, the
government can search any home they like and even
seize personal property. Do you want all your video
games to be taken away?'

In the years that followed, calls to democratise
the territory got louder with every Handover
anniversary – an annual reminder of the city's slow
decline since its reversion to Chinese rule. Senior
leadership in Beijing needed to quell public anger in
Hong Kong before they lost their grip on the city.
In 2007 China's central legislative body – the Standing Committee of the National People's Congress
(NPC) – found a quick fix. They made a promise to
the people of Hong Kong that they would be given
the right to freely elect the chief executive by 2017,
and all members of LegCo by 2020. It would mean
that Hong Kongers could choose their leaders and

their democratic representatives for the first time in history.

If kept, this promise would be the single biggest step towards Hong Kong's democratisation. Even though the Basic Law guarantees universal suffrage as an 'eventual goal', it is silent on when and how this goal should be fulfilled. The 2007 promise answered at least the question of 'when'.

The 'how' question, on the other hand, continued to make many in the pro-democracy camp uneasy. Still, Hong Kongers can have a short memory and an even shorter attention span. By the time the national education saga unfolded in 2012, most citizens had forgotten all about the NPC promise. Even SARS had become ancient history.

The first person to recognise both the necessity and the urgency of working out the details of electoral reform was Professor Benny Tai, a respected expert in constitutional law. I met Professor Tai during the anti-national education campaign in 2012, when he would come to our protests to show support as an academic. We didn't get to know each other too well back then but I had a strong feeling that our paths would cross again soon.

In late 2013, four years before the first prong of the 2007 promise was to be delivered, the Hong

Kong government announced the initial round of public consultations to discuss the mechanics of the 2017 election of the chief executive.* In the following spring, Professor Tai, sociology professor Chan Kin-man and Baptist minister Reverend Chu Yiu-ming threatened a civil disobedience campaign if the government refused to listen to people. They called it Occupy Central with Love and Peace (OCLP).

The so-called 'Occupy Central Trio' proposed a mass sit-in at the heart of the city's financial district if Beijing were to renege on its promise or sabotage the chief executive election by pre-screening candidates, or introducing unreasonable nomination criteria. The non-violent campaign would paralyse business activities, the very lifeblood of Hong Kong's DNA. To make their threat credible, the Occupy Central Trio even picked a venue and date: Chater Garden, 1 October. Expected turnout: 3,000.

Along with my Scholarism colleagues, I watched the unfolding events with great interest. If universal suffrage was the answer to all of society's problems, then we students wanted to be a part of

---

* On 26 March 2017, Beijing's preferred candidate Carrie Lam was elected chief executive under the current, highly restricted, electoral design.

that solution. Professor Tai and I appeared together in several high-profile media interviews to discuss how the fight for universal suffrage might play out in the coming months.

In June the Occupy Central Trio organised an unofficial eight-day citywide referendum, posing to the general public three alternative methods for carrying out the 2017 chief executive election. The most progressive of the three options was jointly proposed by us at Scholarism and the Hong Kong Federation of Students in the hope of nudging us closer to our promised universal suffrage. It was the only option that insisted on a feature called 'civil nomination', which would allow individual citizens to nominate candidates in order to circumvent any pre-screening by Beijing. I had been the first to pro-pose civil nomination in 2013 when the public consultation began and had been its most vocal advocate ever since. In all, 800,000 citizens – one in nine Hong Kongers – participated in the poll, casting their votes at physical ballot boxes set up on univer-sity campuses or via a smartphone app.

Although civil society could talk about civil nomination and other fancy features all we wanted, ultimately it was Beijing that called the shots. On 31 August the NPC Standing Committee issued their own definitive framework for the election. It capped the number of candidates for the chief executive post at 'two to three' and required each candidate to be selected by a 1,200-member nominating committee, in much the same way as our past chief executives had been chosen. Beijing had found a way to present us with what looked like universal suffrage – without giving it to us at all.

Sitting in our rented office, I and other Scholarism members watched the announcement of this 31 August framework in disbelief and disgust. 'That's why my parents tell me never to trust the Communists,' I confided to Agnes Chow. I felt like someone had just kicked my stomach, 1,200 times.

Hours after the announcement a teary-eyed Professor Tai appeared at a hastily organised press conference. 'Today is the darkest day of Hong Kong's democratic development,' he said. 'Our dialogue with Beijing has reached the end of the road.' He told his supporters that he had no choice but to press ahead with the Occupy Central campaign on 1 October.

Professor Tai might have been heartbroken but I was downright furious. The people of Hong Kong had waited seven years for nothing. Beijing's version of electoral reform was as much a walk-back on its promise as it was an insult to our intelligence. The 31 August framework was an open taunt to Hong Kongers: too bad, so sad.

And what are you going to do about it?

I knew I wasn't the only one who did want to do something about it. Empowered and emboldened by our anti-national education campaign from two years ago, students were among the first to act on their outrage over the NPC bombshell. While the Occupy Central Trio were still busy running rehearsals and workshops in preparation for their 1 October launch, student groups like Scholarism felt we had to take matters into our own hands. Instead of waiting for the adults to act, we fired the first shot and set off a chain of events that would change the course of our history.

Two weeks after the NPC announcement, on 13 September, I led Scholarism in a mass demonstration in Admiralty outside the government headquarters. We called on participants to wear a yellow ribbon as a show of solidarity with our cause.

The following week, the Hong Kong Federation of Students, headed by Alex Chow, Lester Shum and Nathan Law, announced a five-day class boycott at all eight of Hong Kong's universities and staged massive student assemblies on various campuses. To find strength in numbers, the HKFS subsequently moved its on-campus demonstrations to Admiralty to merge with ours. Likewise, Scholarism extended the HKFS citywide class boycott to secondary schools across the city. By the end of September our joined-up campaign had been staging daily sit-ins in Admiralty and the crowds surpassed 10,000.

It all came to a head on Friday 26 September. At a meeting between Scholarism and HKFS that afternoon, Nathan raised the concern that had been on everyone's mind for some time. 'The government has grown used to our banners and slogans: we need an escalation plan.' We were sitting in a circle behind a makeshift stage set up outside Civic Square, as it was now widely known, the very place where only two years ago I had delivered the speech of my life.

For weeks, on the pretext of public safety, Civic Square had been walled off with a 10-foot fence by the police, turning it into an intimidating fortress. My eyes were trained on the fence surrounding the square when an idea came to me. 'Tonight, we will reclaim Civic Square,' I said.

By sundown, nearly 10,000 citizens had gathered outside the government headquarters, as they had every night for the past two weeks. For hours, student activists took turns going up on stage to give rousing speeches demanding immediate government action to address our call for universal suffrage. At around 10.30pm, Nathan handed me the microphone and I called on the crowd to occupy Civic Square. Hundreds of demonstrators answered my call and rushed towards the fence and began climbing over into the square. Within minutes law enforcement arrived and responded with pepper spray. As I was clambering up the fence, from out of nowhere I was pulled down by the police and arrested on the spot. My glasses fell off my face and one of my trainers slipped off as I was carried by my arms and legs through the crowd by eight officers to a police vehicle. I couldn't see, I was kicking and screaming, and I had no idea where I was. The following day, Alex and Lester were arrested and taken into custody.

It was the first time I had been arrested – I was 17 years old. I was taken to a detention cell at the nearby police headquarters where I would spend the next 46 hours cut off from the outside world. The tiny cell had no windows and no furniture other than a bench. For two whole days I subsisted on tap water, inedible food and hardly any sleep. I couldn't see clearly without my glasses and, with only one shoe on, I had to limp as I was taken by the police from one room to the next for questioning. Numerous officers asked to take my statement and video my interrogation. I didn't know what to say and so I said nothing like the suspects do in crime movies. One of the guards sneered at me, 'You could have stayed in school but you chose to be a troublemaker. How much money did the Americans give you to do this?' I felt alone, helpless and incredibly guilty – I couldn't bring myself to think how worried my parents must feel not knowing what had happened to their son.

By the time I was released on bail, it was the early morning of 29 September. After a long shower at home, I turned on the television to see what I had missed. I learned that within 24 hours of my arrest, the number of protesters in Admiralty had surged to nearly 200,000. My jaw dropped when I saw powerful images of tear gas being deployed by riot police outside the government headquarters and unarmed demonstrators using nothing but umbrellas, rain ponchos, cling film and other household objects to fend off pepper spray and tear gas. 'This isn't the Hong Kong I know,' I thought to myself, shaking my head while the same footage looped on the 24-hour news channel.

As it turned out, the tear gas crackdown on 28 September was precisely the shock needed to jolt the adults into action. That same night, Professor Tai took to the stage in Admiralty and fired the shot that he should have fired weeks ago: 'Occupy Central officially begins!' he declared. That was the start of the 79-day occupy movement that the foreign press dubbed the 'Umbrella Revolution'.

The movement didn't happen in a social vacuum. The broken promise of electoral reform and subsequent police crackdown catalysed the unrest, but they didn't cause it. It took decades of pent-up frustration over income inequality, social immobility and other injustices for public anger to finally boil over. Martin Luther King Jr famously said that freedom is never voluntarily given by the oppressor and that it must be demanded by the oppressed. The Umbrella Movement was our way of making our demands heard.

The Umbrella Movement had not only put Hong Kong on the map, it had also brought out the absolute best in us. Everywhere we looked we saw citizens of all ages and professions handing out free food, water and medical supplies to protesters. Office workers showed up during their lunch breaks with cash donations; parents and retirees took shifts to manage the provisions; students sat for civic lessons that no class could teach them. The crowds at the three main sites – Admiralty, Mongkok and Causeway Bay – were ten times bigger than those at the anti-national education campaign. The movement's symbol, the yellow umbrella, captured both the humility and humanity of the non-violent protesters.

On 1 October, China's National Day, I called on everyone to bring tents and blankets in preparation for a prolonged struggle. Shortly after, a tent city emerged on Harcourt Road as protesters began to spend the night in the world's largest outdoor sleep-over. To support a self-sustaining community, amenities like supply stations and medical centres grew up like mushrooms. I was particularly inspired by a makeshift library made out of donated marquees and furniture, where row upon row of secondary school students, still wearing their uniforms, read and did homework under the supervision of volunteer tutors. 'You think that's impressive?' Agnes said to me. 'You should see the women's toilets. There are more skincare and cosmetic products than a department store. And they are all free!' The Western press called us the world's politest protesters, but in my mind we were also its most resourceful, creative and disciplined.

Still, defying Communist China was hardly fun and games. Although law enforcement had pulled back after being widely condemned for the tear-gas crackdown, within days hired thugs began to descend on protest sites. The situation was especially tense in Mongkok, a rough-and-tumble working-class enclave on the other side of the Victoria Harbour. Reports of physical altercations and even sexual assault began to appear on online news sites and caused unease among protesters over their personal safety. 'My mum just called and begged me to go home,' Agnes said. 'The mobs are trying to scare not only the protesters but also their parents!'

I woke up one morning in my tent on Tim Mei Avenue – the camping ground for Scholarism and the HKFS – soaked to the bone. Someone had sneaked into my tent while I was sleeping and cut open a water bottle. I ruled out the possibility that the act was a practical joke as nobody was in the mood for pranks.

Actual and threatened violence was coupled with verbal intimidation. Since the class boycott in September, accusations against student activists that they were receiving support from foreign governments had been swirling on Chinese state media. Pro-Beijing politicians in Hong Kong had gone on television and radio talk shows slinging mud against Alex, Nathan and me, trumping up conspiracy theories about our supposed connections to the CIA and MI6. Even ordinary citizens weren't immune from this so-called 'white terror'. For fear of upsetting the Chinese government, many companies forbade their staff from visiting protest zones or showing support for protesters on social media.

As the movement dragged on, cracks started to show within the loose coalition of student activists, the Occupy Central Trio and veteran pro-democracy politicians. The challenge of a largely leaderless movement – the Occupy Central Trio and student activists like myself were the faces of the movement but hardly its commanders – was that it was often difficult, if not impossible, to reach consensus among multiple stakeholders. Weeks could fly by without any decision being made or action being taken. Other than one televised debate between student activists and senior government officials in mid-October that resulted in no resolutions, neither side had moved an inch. Every day, protesters alternated between pushing back the police on the frontlines on the one hand, and doing homework and feeding themselves on the other. The protest sites became a bubble isolating the campers from the outside world. As the autumn chills set in, the movement continued to drift further and further away from its original goal of electoral reform.

Unhappy with the lack of progress, splinter groups calling themselves 'localists' began to coalesce. They were particularly irritated by the 'kumbaya' atmosphere in Admiralty and viewed our coalition with as much disdain as they did the government. Their attempts to break into government buildings were foiled by moderate protesters, which only deepened the discord. Just as the movement had polarised society into so-called 'yellow ribbons' (pro-occupy) and 'blue ribbons' (pro-police and government), the movement itself had been split into moderates and radicals. This played right into the hands of C.Y. Leung and his bosses in Beijing, who had hoped that a war of attrition would lead to division and infighting, which would in turn weaken and eventually destroy the movement.

That was exactly what happened. By late November, two months after the first shot of tear gas was fired, pro-Beijing trade groups succeeded in obtaining court orders to clear the protest zones on the grounds that campers were disrupting business activities. Bailiffs and removal crews began dismantling barricades and tents, often with the help of police officers and even thugs. Meanwhile, protesters didn't put up much of a fight, in part because they didn't want to defy the court, and in part because they themselves knew that the movement had to come to an end one way or another.

Still, some of us refused to give in just yet. On 25 November, Lester Shum and I were among several activists arrested in Mongkok for violating a court injunction to stay clear of the protest zone. While being carried off by the police, I shouted, 'Why are you doing this? We are fighting for you and your children too!' It was my second arrest. After spending 30 hours in a cell, I appeared in front of a judge and was charged with contempt of court.

In the coming days, one after another the protest sites began to fall to excavators and dump trucks. On 15 December, bailiffs cleared the last camping ground in Causeway Bay, bringing to an end 79 days of student-led street occupation. Even though the movement failed to deliver the political results it set out to achieve, the sweeping political awakening and civic engagement it brought about are indisputable. It was a paradigm shift that reshaped and continues to reshape the political landscape in Hong Kong, forever altering the relationship between state and citizens, the oppressor and the oppressed. Like the anti-national education campaign in 2012, the Umbrella Movement gave Hong Kongers, especially my generation, new confidence to challenge Communist China.

For me, the biggest takeaway from the movement had nothing to do with the question of success or failure. Even the harshest critic must acknowledge that it was the first popular uprising in Hong Kong and that we had neither a precedent to rely on nor a manual to follow. We did the best we could under the circumstances.

What mattered was what we would do with this transformative experience. The movement might have ended with the dismantling of the last protest site, but its legacy and spirit would live on. It had to, because our struggle was far from over. We needed to turn our frustration into resolve and motivation, and rebuild our trust and respect for each other.

Towards the end of the Occupy Wall Street campaign in the US in 2011, Slovenian philosopher Slavoj Žižek addressed the crowd in Zuccotti Park:

> All we need is patience. The only thing I'm afraid of is that we will someday just go home and then we will meet once a year, drinking beer, and nostalgically remember what a nice time we had here. Promise yourselves that this will not be the case. We know that people often desire something but do not really want it. Don't be afraid to really want what you desire.

We could use some of that fighting spirit right about now.

From Protesters to Politicians: The Founding of Demosistō

從抗爭者到政治人物: 香港眾志的創立

I was the student activist who organised the first series of mass protests in the lead-up to the Umbrella Movement and the first to be arrested for actions relating to it. My role as a teenage revolutionary captured the imagination of the international community and became a teachable moment for young activists the world over. Whereas the national education campaign made me a household name in Hong Kong, the Umbrella Movement turned me into a global poster boy for resistance against Communist China.

In October 2014, *Time* magazine put me on the cover of its international edition next to the headline THE FACE OF PROTEST. Within the same month, I penned my first *New York Times* op-ed, titled 'Taking Back Hong Kong's Future'. By then, every media outlet from every corner of the world had descended on the protest zone on Harcourt Road seeking an interview. I was named Young Person of the Year 2014 by *The Times* and ranked tenth on the World's 50 Greatest Leaders list by *Fortune* magazine. 'If I had known *Time* would use that picture on the cover, I would have got a haircut first,' I joked to my parents.

In truth, I never asked for fame, and I certainly didn't do what I did to get famous. As much as I was humbled and often embarrassed by the overwhelming media attention, I wanted to harness it and turn it into political capital for our pro-democracy struggle. At the first post-Umbrella Movement Scholarism meeting in 2015, I said to a roomful of our activists, 'Recent events have awakened many Hong Kongers and we must transform every ounce of that new energy into ballots.' The Umbrella Movement had taught us many important lessons; one of them was that fighting on the streets alone wasn't enough. We needed to change the political system from within, and we would do that by sending young people into the legislature. We had to beat the government at their own game.

To do that, we needed a new platform that would appeal not just to students – I'd recently graduated from secondary school and was in my first year at the Open University – but also adult voters who were motivated by a different set of priorities and concerns.

In April 2016, 17 months after the last protest zone was cleared, we relaunched Scholarism as Demosistō, a youth political party. The name is a portmanteau of the Greek for 'people' and the Latin for 'I stand'.

Our launch was hardly smooth: the press conference started several hours late due to a microphone malfunction and the live streaming on YouTube was interrupted so many times that the number of viewers dropped at one point from a few hundred to below 20. Localist groups that had been critical of us poked fun at our name (they said it sounded like 'Demolition') and accused us of selling out to become greasy politicians. But as Nathan reminded me after the rocky press conference, democracy is a process. Part of it is to win over those who don't like us. Remembering this made me feel a whole lot better.

As soon as Demosistō heaved into life, we plunged ourselves into preparing for the 2016 legislative council election, which was only five months away. There was unanimous support within the party for Nathan Law to run, not only because he was old enough to do so (Agnes and I were both one year shy of the minimum nomination age of 21), but also because he possessed the perfect blend of temperament, maturity and public profile we were looking for in our candidate.

We agreed to run on a platform of 'self-determination'. Under the Basic Law, the one-country, two systems framework – and thus the city's semi-autonomy – would expire in 2047. At that point we believed that Hong Kongers should be given a say to determine their own destiny by means of a referendum, in contrast to what happened during the Handover discussions when Britain and China negotiated our future without our participation.

Self-determination is an established concept in international law and is a recognised human right in the United Nations International Covenant on Civil and Political Rights. But it was a new concept in Hong Kong, and newer still to the pro-Beijing camp, which often falsely accused Demosistō of advocating independence or a colour revolution.

Election campaigns are backbreaking work for any political party, especially one with limited resources and an unhelpful student union image to shake. Unlike well-funded pro-Beijing parties, Demosistō relies solely on crowdfunding and public donations we collect from street rallies. Despite Nathan's boy-next-door appeal, his poll numbers hovered between a measly 1 to 3 per cent, even down to the final month. 'Why are our numbers so low?' we asked each other in disbelief every morning when we checked the news.

We learned the hard way that likeability doesn't always translate into electability, especially in Nathan's Hong Kong Island constituency, which consists mostly of well-educated professionals and affluent business elites – many of whom would almost always choose stability over freedom, profit over principle.

Compared to his opponents, Nathan's youth was a handicap and his leadership role in the Umbrella Movement was an original sin that turned off the protest-fatigued middle class. 'We've put every last cent we have into this campaign. If we lose, we'll be left with nothing,' Nathan said to me on the one-month countdown to Election Day.

In a superhero movie, the situation always looks the most hopeless before the good guys bounce back to save the day. In our case, we hit that point of inflexion less than three weeks before voters headed to the ballot box, when even friendly media outlets had all but written us off. After a series of stellar televised debate performances, Nathan's poll numbers started to rise. 'Yellow ribbon' celebrities like

Cantopop singers Anthony Wong and Denise Ho –
who both figured prominently during the Umbrella
Movement – offered their endorsement. Our outside-
the-box marketing campaign using Instagram Live
and virtual reality videos, managed by our chief
media officer Ivan Lam, generated massive buzz
on social media. In the final month before Election
Day, Demosistians were on the streets every night
past midnight handing out flyers and greeting
voters. We were by far the hardest working political
party in all of Hong Kong. 'You guys are working
even harder than you did during Umbrella and that's
saying a lot!' my mum would complain to me, as she
had to put up with my late nights and endless strategising with fellow Demosistians. Still, we clenched
our teeth and pressed ahead. The Chinese saying
that diligence can make up for all shortcomings was
still keeping me going.

Shortly after midnight on 4 September, after
the voting booths had closed and the ballots counted,
the results were in: Nathan won over 50,000 votes
and, at 23 years old, became the youngest ever
elected legislator in Asia. Every Demosistian at the
counting station broke down in tears of joy, even
Agnes who is the hardiest among us. Five gruelling months of crashing overnight at our messy
campaign room and standing for days on street

corners under the punishing sun had finally paid off. Wiping away my tears, I gave Nathan a bear hug and said, 'We did it!'

As the city's only student lawmaker, Nathan entered LegCo with a clear mandate. He would focus his efforts on education reform, youth employment and housing policy. As an avid video gamer and semi-professional e-sports commentator, Nathan also wanted to position Hong Kong as a hub for international video-game competitions, although privately he acknowledged that this was more a pet project than a priority on his political agenda.

Nathan's LegCo seat was barely warm when a constitutional crisis, dubbed 'Oathgate', blew up and eventually cost him his job. At the swearing-in ceremony in October, half-a-dozen freshmen legislators, including Nathan, strayed from their oath to make a political statement. When he swore his allegiance to China, Nathan modified his tone on the last word in the sentence, essentially transforming the pledge into a question.

It had been a tradition within the pro-democracy camp to use the oath-taking ceremony as a platform of protest by displaying props, shouting slogans or adding words to the prescribed oath. But this time, in an act of mission creep to rid the legislature of unwanted newcomers, the government brought legal action to remove the six lawmakers for their antics.

Beijing gladly played along and issued an interpretation of the Basic Law that concurred with the government's position. In a decision issued in November, the NPC Standing Committee ruled that if a legislator-elect 'deliberately fails to take an oath in the correct way, he or she cannot retake it and shall be disqualified from assuming public office'.

Oathgate dragged on for months as the legal action initiated by the government moved through the court systems. In July 2017, ten months after Nathan's history-making election win, the court ruled against the six lawmakers in deference to the NPC. If ousting them wasn't bad enough, the government then had the audacity to demand that they pay back their salaries and expense reimbursements. Even my mum couldn't hold back her anger. 'I voted for Nathan last September,' she said. 'Who gives the government the right to invalidate my vote? And what kind of employer makes their employees return their pay after firing them?'

Nathan hit rock bottom. Not only had he lost his hard-earned seat, he and I were about to begin our trial for our roles in the Umbrella Movement. 'I'm out of a job and may need to file for bankruptcy if I have to cough back my salary. On top of that, you and I may have to go to prison in a few weeks. How will Demosistō survive all of this?' he said, his eyes all cried out and unseeing. Though he was inconsolable, I tried to comfort him. 'If we survived the worst of the Umbrella Movement, we will survive this too.'

Local commentators often likened the situation of post-Handover Hong Kong to a boiling frog. According to the metaphor, if a frog is put in tepid water which is then slowly brought to a boil, it won't notice the gradual change in temperature and will unknowingly be cooked to death. Beijing has been chipping away at Hong Kong's freedoms for years without us noticing. Since 1997, the Chinese Communist Party has been co-opting local business leaders in Hong Kong to buy up and exert influence over print-media outlets, bookshop chains, publishing houses and radio and television stations. This so-called 'United Front' campaign was designed by Beijing to tighten control on Hong Kong society while quietly implementing its own political agenda in the increasingly embattled semi-autonomous territory.

But that was then and this is now. Since 2014 the Chinese leadership appears no longer in the mood for subtle, creeping changes. In late 2015, for instance, five members of a local publishing house known for printing political 'tell-all' books about the Chinese Communist Party, went missing. They are believed to have been abducted and detained by mainland Chinese agents.

Incidents like the bookseller abductions and Oathgate are signs that Beijing is losing its patience and increasingly resorting to blunt suppression. It has turned the heat way up and put a lid over the pot. The frog can kick and scream all it wants but there is no escape from the boiling water. That's how it feels to be a Hong Konger these days.

And the bad news keeps coming. They say revenge is a dish best served cold: the Department of Justice waited three years after the Umbrella Movement to charge Nathan, Alex and I with unlawful assembly in relation to the storming of Civic Square on that fateful September night in 2014. On 17 August 2017, two months before my 21st birthday, the court sentenced each of us to six to eight months in jail – by far my longest stint yet – and in doing so made us some of the first prisoners of conscience in the city's history.

Political imprisonment is an inevitable step on the path to democracy – it was the case in South Korea and Taiwan and it's now also the case in Hong Kong. The three of us know that first-hand. Far from silencing us, however, jail would only strengthen our resolve.

ACT II

INCARCERATION: LETTERS FROM PIK UK

Things can't defeated us can make us stronger.

Facsimile of letter written by Joshua from Pik Uk Prison, 19 August 2017.

Letter from Pik Uk Correctional Institution

獄中的信

Day 2 – Friday, 18 August 2017

I've been closely following the news in the daily papers and on the communal radio. I'd like to thank my supporters for their good wishes.

Prison life isn't easy. But that's exactly why I wanted to write you this letter and many more in the coming months. I want to share with you the thoughts that have been churning inside my head and to let you know that I'm thinking of all of you on the other side of these prison walls.

The last words I said before I was taken away from the courtroom were 'Hong Kong people, carry on!' That sums up how I feel about our political struggle.

In March 2013, Professor Benny Tai announced his Occupy Central campaign. His goal was to demand universal suffrage by paralysing our financial district – the most effective way to make our government listen. Professor Tai had warned us that imprisonment would be the final and inevitable step in a civil disobedience campaign.

Since Occupy Central – and the Umbrella Movement that succeeded it – ended without achieving its stated goal, Hong Kong has entered one of its most challenging chapters. Civil society has been stuck in a rut, not knowing whether or how to proceed. Protesters coming out of a failed movement are overcome with disillusionment and powerlessness. Some of them have decided to leave politics altogether, others, like myself, have ended up in prison.

The appeal sentencing of myself and my fellow Umbrella leaders Nathan Law and Alex Chow by the Court of Appeal has dealt yet another devastating blow to the morale of pro-democracy activists. So too has the conviction of the so-called 'NNT Thirteen' – 13 activists who clashed with police during a protest against a controversial government development project in the north-eastern New Territories near the Chinese border.

Even though it feels like we have hit rock bottom, we need to stay true to our cause. We must. To my friends who have decided to walk away from politics, I hope my being here and writing you this letter will convince you to reconsider. If not, our sacrifices – the loss of freedom by all 16 of us – will have been for nothing.

I want to tell you about everything that has happened to me at Pik Uk since my incarceration 36 hours ago. I'm glad to report that so far I haven't experienced any mistreatment by prison authorities. I hope it will stay this way until the day I walk out of this place. Being a new inmate, I'm required to go through a ten-day orientation. My actual prison routine won't start for a few days and I haven't got the faintest idea what's in store for me and whether I can handle it. Things do seem stricter than I expected from a juvenile prison. For instance, all inmates must learn military-style drill commands and march early every morning. It makes me wonder if Nathan and Alex are required to do the same in their adult prisons.

To my surprise, the meals aren't so bad – far better than what they fed us during our detention at the police station. That being said, I miss my mum's hand-brewed milk tea terribly, and the chicken hotpot at the street-food restaurant where my friends and I always hang out at. That's the first place I'll visit as soon as I'm out of here.

There are two things I'm going to really struggle to get used to here: the monotony and the absolute authority of those in charge. I need to make sure I don't let either of these dull my critical thinking or stop me from challenging the authorities the way I've always done. I plan to use my 'downtime' to figure out the way forward and find better ways to work with the rest of civil society to make full democracy a reality. I know I have to keep my mind occupied in prison or else prison will occupy my mind instead.

Tomorrow morning I'll speak to my welfare officer and request a subscription to the liberal *Ming Pao* and *Apple Daily* – the only two credible broadsheet newspapers left in Hong Kong – to stay informed of what's happening in the outside world. I'll also request a radio to listen to the morning and evening phone-in radio programmes. Without these things, time will crawl and life behind bars will be all the more unbearable.

That said, whatever I'm going through is nothing compared to the false imprisonment of Liu Xiaobo in mainland China or the illegal detention of the bookseller Lam Wing-kee.* These men are an

---

* Liu Xiaobo, a Chinese human rights activist and winner of the 2010 Nobel Peace Prize, was sentenced to 11 years in prison for co-authoring a manifesto calling for political pluralism in China. He died from liver cancer in 2017 while incarcerated. Lam Wing-kee was one of the five Causeway

inspiration and a reminder that I need all the inner strength I can muster to get through the next six months. As long as I continue to read and write I will be able to keep my mind free. The great Mahatma Gandhi once said: 'You can chain me, you can torture me, you can even destroy this body, but you will never imprison my mind.' Gandhi's words have now taken on much more personal meaning for me.

At the moment, my biggest worry is the state of my political party. Ever since Nathan and I co-founded Demosistō in April 2016 we've suffered a series of significant setbacks. Four weeks ago, Nathan lost his hard-won seat at the Legislative Council (LegCo) after he and five other members were disqualified on the grounds that they had failed to properly recite their oaths during the swearing-in ceremony. The so-called 'Oathgate' was a ploy by the ruling elite to remove pro-democracy lawmakers from the legislature and redraw the balance of power in local politics.

Nathan's disqualification has dealt a serious blow to Demosistō. Not only has it cost us our only seat in LegCo, but the loss of Nathan's lawmaker

Bay Books booksellers abducted by Chinese authorities for publishing exposés about the Communist leadership (*see page 63–4*).

salary means that our party has lost its sole source of steady income. We were given a week to pack up and vacate the LegCo Building. Nathan and his staff – all of whom are Demosistō members – became instantly unemployed.

Then, within the same week, three core party members including myself, Nathan and Ivan Lam, all went to jail. Nathan and I were each sentenced to six months over the storming of Civic Square two days before the eruption of the Umbrella Movement, and Ivan was one of the NNT Thirteen. In the meantime, Derek Lam, another core member, will go to trial this week for his role in another protest outside the Hong Kong Liaison Office – the de facto Chinese embassy in Hong Kong and the mastermind behind many controversial policies put forward by our government.

Nearly everyone at Demosistō is now out of a job and must find ways to keep the party afloat, while half of our executive committee is behind bars, or will be in the coming weeks. I sometimes joke that soon there will be enough of us in prison to have quorum for a committee meeting.

I can't think of another political party in Hong Kong that has gone through as many ups and downs as Demosistō has in the last 15 months. It must be disheartening and disorienting for party members, especially young graduates who have recently joined us. But as much as we moan about everything we've been through, I believe our trials and tribulations are precisely what we need to grow and prosper. As they say, 'only through fire is a strong sword forged'. Indeed, all the speed bumps we've gone over have only made us stronger and more prepared for even bigger challenges that lie ahead. After all, if we can get through the anti-national education campaign and the Umbrella Movement, we can survive anything.

And my message to the pro-Beijing camp? Don't celebrate too soon. Demosistō will use everything we've got to win back Nathan's seat in the upcoming by-elections. What we lack in financial resources, we more than make up for in determination. Hong Kong voters don't suffer fools gladly. They see right through your tricks and will send one of us right back into LegCo.

I will end by sharing with you my state of mind during the sentence hearing yesterday. Walking into the High Court, I was moved beyond words by the hundreds of supporters who had come out to cheer us on. Inside the courtroom, there was a gathering of like-minded friends who have stood by us at every step of the way through our legal battles. When the judges handed down our sentences, some of those friends broke into tears, others chanted slogans. People clapped their hands and stomped their feet – it got so loud that the judge pounded his gavel and ordered silence in court. I knew then that I was not, and would never be, alone on this journey.

I began my journey in 2012 when I led the campaign against the national education curriculum. It's been a tumultuous five years. I didn't shed a single tear when the judge announced my sentence, not because I was brave but because I wanted my supporters to embrace my loss of freedom as a necessary step on our collective path to democracy. To quote J.K. Rowling: 'What's coming will come and we'll meet it when it does.'

Hong Kong is at a crossroads. The ruling regime will stop at nothing to silence dissent. They have relentlessly pursued and will continue to pursue whomever they consider a threat to their grip on power. For those who dare to stand up to them, the only way forward is together. And tonight, alone in my cell, I ask you to keep your chin up and use your tears, anger and frustration as motivation to charge ahead.

Hong Kong people, carry on!

The Situation Outside Is More Dire Than the One Inside

監倉外的形勢比監倉內更嚴峻

Day 3 – Saturday, 19 August 2017

I've been assigned a two-person cell. My cellmate seems friendly enough, although we didn't have a chance to say much to each other before the lights went out last night.

Conditions in a juvenile prison cell aren't as bad as I thought. Even though summer is in full swing the air circulation is acceptable and the heat is tolerable. So far the biggest source of discomfort is perhaps the bed. In fact, calling it a bed is an overstatement. It's nothing more than a wooden plank with no mattress. But, then again, if I could spend 79 nights sleeping on a highway during the Umbrella Movement I'm sure I can get used to this too.

Prison is all about discipline and following orders. Every morning we have to get up at 6am sharp and every night the lights go out at 10pm.

Even when I was campaigning for Nathan in his 2016 bid for LegCo I didn't have to get up that early. I guess I'm not a morning person.

Twice a day, the news is broadcast on the PA system. This morning I was woken up by a story about Chris Patten, the last Governor of Hong Kong. 'At a public appearance,' the news presenter said, 'Mr Patten told reporters that he was heartened by the sacrifices made by Joshua Wong, Alex Chow and Nathan Law, and that he believed these three names will be carved into history . . .' It felt surreal to hear my name mentioned in this way in front of other inmates. The reality that I'm a convicted criminal has finally sunk in.

As far as I understand it, inmates are permitted to subscribe to their own newspapers. Other than that, there are so-called 'communal papers' that we can borrow and read for free. To my dismay (although I shouldn't be surprised), most of them are pro-Beijing mouthpieces like *Wen Wei Po*, *Ta Kung Pao* and *Sing Tao Daily*.

Luckily, I managed to borrow a copy of *Apple Daily* from another inmate. That's how I learned about the outpouring of public support for the 'Umbrella Trio' of me, Alex and Nathan and the wall-to-wall coverage of our imprisonment by the foreign press.

I hope what happened to the three of us will send a clear message to the international community: the rule of law in Hong Kong is crumbling and gradually turning into a 'rule *by* law'. Strict compliance now trumps personal liberty and peaceful calls for democracy. Our government's relentless pursuit of political activists through the criminal justice system not only violates freedom of expression, it also blurs the lines that separate the three branches of government – executive, legislative and judicial – and ultimately erodes our trust in the city's independent judiciary.

In many ways, the situation on the other side of these prison walls is far more dire than it is inside. I count on everyone who loves and cares about Hong Kong, whether they live here or abroad, to continue the fight in my absence. They say what doesn't kill us makes us stronger. Once we get through this round of political prosecution, we'll pick ourselves up and be more united than ever.

As soon as I finish my orientation I'll be assigned to an inmate work group. Until then I'll be doing simple tasks like sweeping the canteen floor, folding laundry and shining shoes. In the coming months I'll write frequently. I'll look after myself and keep my friends and family in my thoughts.

Looking for Answers in Juvenile Prison

在少年監獄尋找答案

Day 4 – Sunday, 20 August 2017

Prison life follows a strict timetable. Sunday is our 'day off', when inmates get to hang out at the canteen for the entire day between seven in the morning and seven in the evening.

'Hanging out' would be torturous if it wasn't for the TV. For most inmates, one of the highlights on Sunday is watching soap-opera reruns on TVB (Television Broadcasts Limited, the only free-to-air television network in Hong Kong) in the afternoon. Never mind that TVB is hugely unpopular because of its near-monopoly on broadcasting and its pro-Beijing, pro-government bias in everything it airs, from news reporting to programme selection. In prison, I suppose some entertainment is better than no entertainment.

I was happy to see fellow Umbrella Movement student leader Lester Shum appear live on TVB's current affairs programme *On the Record* talking about political imprisonment. There was also news coverage of another Sunday afternoon mass protest in support of the Umbrella Trio. Other than watching television, I killed time by reading my borrowed copy of yesterday's *Apple Daily* cover to cover.

Apart from the mattressless bed, the hardest thing (pun intended) to get used to here is being cut off from the outside world. It's one thing to have zero access to social media like Facebook and Twitter, but quite another to have zero conversations with friends. So I savour every opportunity to feel a sense of connection with the outside world, whether it's through the television, the radio or newspapers.

The most exciting thing that happened today was when I saw Ivan Lam mentioned on the evening news. The presenter read excerpts from a letter Ivan had written from his prison cell. Even though we were put in different prisons (Correctional Services always separates prisoners who know each other to avoid organised actions in prison), hearing Ivan's words instantly made me feel like he was here sitting next to me.

Over the last couple of days I've made a few friends at Pik Uk. Today I chatted with a fellow young prisoner of conscience, Mak Tze-hei. In March 2017, when he was 20 years old, Tze-hei was convicted of rioting for his role in the 2016 Mongkok Chinese New Year civil unrest* and sentenced to two years in prison. What I quickly realised was that even though our political views are different (he's a pro-independence firebrand and I'm not), we can still have a free and meaningful exchange of ideas. After all, we've both ended up behind bars for our political beliefs. Most importantly, we share the same love for our city.

Meeting Tze-hei reminded me of the many forgotten activists who have received neither the fame nor the public support that myself, Nathan and Alex enjoy and sometimes take for granted. Not being a household name makes it much harder for them to get funding to receive the best legal representation. We need to draw attention to the fact that there are scores of unsung heroes, from those who took part

---

* Nicknamed the 'Fish-ball Revolution' by the local press, on Chinese New Year's Eve in February 2016, hundreds of protesters, most of them localists who advocated Hong Kong independence, clashed with riot police after the government cracked down on unlicensed but popular food vendors in Mongkok (many of whom sold fish-balls). Scores of protesters were charged with rioting.

in the Mongkok unrest to those in the NNT Thirteen, who are struggling in silence.

On the subject of forgotten activists, today I also met a number of protesters who had taken part in the Umbrella Movement and the anti-national education demonstrations. I haven't yet had the chance to find out how they ended up in jail, but I recognised their faces from protests over the years.

The majority of the inmates – roughly 70 per cent by my estimate – are convicted on drug-related charges, some of them users, others dealing. Society labels them criminals and *fai ching* (literally 'useless youths' in Cantonese). Few realise that these young people are only symptoms of what has gone wrong with our education and social systems and not the cause. No one is born a criminal.

Mostly I find my fellow inmates genuine and warm. And there is much I can learn from them. In eight weeks' time, I'll turn 21 and be transferred to an adult prison in a different part of town. Until then I'll make a conscious effort to get to know them and hear their stories.

It all brings into sharp focus the hypocrisy of our governing elites. Political leaders like Chief Executive Carrie Lam and Chief Secretary Matthew Cheung are always talking about how much effort they've put into 'engaging the youth' of Hong Kong.

These are the same people who disqualified Nathan and other young lawmakers from LegCo, in doing so nullifying the votes of tens of thousands of young voters. They went on to prosecute youth protesters and throw them in prison. Not once has a single government officer sat down with the activists to try to negotiate a way out of the political impasse.

Earlier today, a young inmate told me that he had met Nathan on a lawmaker's prison visit. In Hong Kong, LegCo members and Justices of the Peace (JPs) – a title of honour bestowed by the government on community leaders – are among the privileged few who can visit any prisoner whenever they want. Before 'Oathgate' took away his seat, Nathan exercised that right and visited a number of prisons, including Pik Uk. The irony that Nathan himself is now behind bars isn't lost on any of us.

Closing Arguments at My Contempt of Court Hearing

旺角清場被捕結案陳詞

Day 8 – Thursday, 24 August 2017

This morning I left Pik Uk to attend the final hearing of my contempt of court case. It was good to have a break from the daily monotony of life in the facility and see a few familiar faces – even if it was only in the courtroom.

I was one of 20 activists charged with contempt after we violated a court injunction to stay clear of the protest zone in Mongkok during the final days of the Umbrella Movement. My lawyers advised me to plead guilty to mitigate my sentence; three to six months seems to be the consensus among them.

With good conduct, the six-month sentence I'm currently serving for storming Civic Square would be shortened by a third to four months, meaning I could be released as early as 17 December were it not for the contempt case. However, the presiding judge will probably combine the two sentences and keep me in detention for a few more months. In all likelihood I'll remain in prison until the end of spring next year. I'm mentally preparing myself for the possibility that I'll be spending both Christmas and Chinese New Year behind bars.

I'm quick to remind myself that other activists have received much harsher sentences than mine. The NNT Thirteen were originally handed community-service orders for storming a LegCo committee meeting in June 2014 before being sentenced to eight to thirteen months in prison after the Department of Justice appealed for harsher punishments. Among them were Ivan and fellow activist Raphael Wong. Raphael is vice chairman of a pro-democracy party called the League of Social Democrats (LSD). The heavy sentences they received set a dangerous precedent for future sentencing of anti-government protesters, which will in turn have a chilling effect on our freedom of assembly in Hong Kong.

I saw Raphael in the courtroom today. He was involved in the same Mongkok contempt of court case. After the hearing, we briefly discussed our appeal strategies with our lawyers should the court rule against us. Raphael was in good spirits as always, despite the triple threat he faces: the

Mongkok contempt trial, the 13-month NNT sentence and, above all, public nuisance charges for his leadership role in the Umbrella Movement.

The whole thing makes me feel a little embarrassed about the enormous media attention that Alex, Nathan and I received last week. Local newspapers plastered my picture on their front pages the day after I was sent to prison. The reality is that countless others are being tried or are about to be tried in Hong Kong for their activism work. Many of them face much harsher prison terms than we do.

On the subject of newspapers, I can't emphasise enough how hard life is without access to news of current events. I'm still trying to get my hands on yesterday's and today's issues of *Ming Pao* and *Apple Daily*, which means I'm at least two days behind on the news. This will remain a daily struggle until my prison subscription begins. I never thought I could crave reading the papers this much – the simple joy of bringing them back to my cell and devouring the local politics section and every opinion column!

I'm used to being constantly on my smartphone, thumbing rapid-fire text messages to friends, shooting off comments to the press and taking care of party matters big and small. Being phoneless is like having my limbs cut off or an itch I can't scratch. I guess I need to learn to let go and get better at delegating party responsibilities to my colleagues. Perhaps I may even learn to enjoy downtime – it seems unlikely but I'll at least try.

I was taken back to Pik Uk in a caged vehicle shortly after lunch. I was told that every inmate is required to take a urine test each time he leaves the prison premises. Until the urine test is cleared we are put in a separate ward away from other inmates. They call it the 'quarantine'.

The next time I leave Pik Uk will be for the sentencing hearing of my contempt case in September, and perhaps again in October if I file an appeal for that sentence. In the meantime, I look forward to receiving letters from loved ones and my first friends-and-family visit this Saturday. The anticipation will keep my spirits up for a few days.

Lawmaker's Visit

議員探訪

Day 9 – Friday, 25 August 2017

LegCo member Shiu Ka-chun came to see me this morning.

Nicknamed 'Bottle',* Shiu is a veteran social worker. He was elected to LegCo in 2016 in the same election in which Nathan won his seat, although the two represented different constituencies. Bottle didn't participate in Oathgate and kept his seat on the council.

Bottle can drop in for a visit any time he wants because of the special privilege enjoyed by lawmakers and Justices of the Peace (*see page 83*). During the one-hour visitation, Bottle discussed his impending public nuisance trial for his leadership

---

* His given name 'Chun' and the word for bottle sound the same in Cantonese.

role in the Umbrella Movement, debriefed me on various meetings within the pan-democratic camp and went through the pan-dem's strategy for the by-elections, in which they hoped to fill the half-dozen seats left empty after Oathgate.

Among the pan-dem lawmakers, Bottle has been the one who pays the most attention to juvenile delinquency. He's known to regularly visit youth prisons like Pik Uk. As expected, he asked me how I was coping behind bars and whether I had experienced any abuse by prison staff. I didn't have anything negative to report because in truth I've been treated fairly well. The other inmates have been friendly towards me and the guards' attitudes have been decent overall. 'If I even sensed a hint of animosity,' I joked to Bottle, 'you bet I would be recording it in my journal!' Joking aside, I know at the back of my mind that we all have Bottle to thank. If it weren't for his tireless efforts over the years to improve prison conditions and raise awareness about prisoner abuse, things could be far worse at Pik Uk.

I met Bottle six years ago, when I was a 14-year-old secondary school student and he a social worker and radio presenter. He later hosted some of my anti-national education rallies. In the documentary Netflix produced about me, *Joshua: Teenager vs*

Superpower, there is a scene in which I appear on Bottle's live radio show and he asks me whether I have a girlfriend. 'My mum told me it's too early for me to be dating,' I reply, and everyone in the studio bursts out laughing. It was a moment of levity. Neither of us would have guessed at the time that five years later we would be talking to each other on different sides of a glass partition.

After Bottle left, I had a bit of time to kill. Due to my quarantine I wasn't allowed to be with the other inmates in the canteen and so I went back to my room for an afternoon nap on that infernal mattressless bed. I can't remember the last time I took an afternoon nap. Once my urine test was cleared, I was told to join the cohort in the common areas. On my way to the main yard I was intercepted by two plainclothes staff who said they wanted me to participate in an inmate survey.

Most of the questions in the survey were pretty mundane:

What crime have you been convicted of?
Do you use drugs?
Are you affiliated with the Triads (organised crime groups)?

Then the questions get more personal:

Are you confident you can find work after your
    release?
Do you consider yourself employable?
Is your family important to you?
Do you have friends you can trust?
Are you in control of your moods and emotions?
Do you have violent tendencies?

I knew that based on the answers to these yes/no
questions I would be assigned to various rehabilitation courses and workshops. I tried not to be cynical
about the methodology because I know that no system is perfect, and I'm sure inmates do benefit from
some of the curriculum. I just can't help but wonder
if the approach is a touch too algorithmic. I also
don't see how they can expect a one-size-fits-all
survey to help them figure out how to re-educate
prisoners of all shapes and sizes. The survey is particularly irrelevant to prisoners of conscience like me
who don't believe they have done anything wrong,
much less wish to repent.

It's Been a While Since I Shook Someone's Hand

久違了的握手

Day 10 – Saturday, 26 August 2017

Time crawls in prison, but the days can also slip through your fingers without you noticing.

It's been ten days since I arrived in Pik Uk, which means my orientation is about to end. Next Monday I'll officially join the other 'graduates' in the group routine, including those dreaded morning marches. I'll also be required to master the intricate art of blanket folding. The task sounds simple but it's tricky for me. During the orientation I barely met the guards' standards even with help from my cellmate. From Monday I'll have to do it on my own and I'm not looking forward to getting an earful from the guards over how clumsy and useless I am.

Beginning next week, my day will be divided into two halves: classes in the morning and work in the afternoon. There are four types of classes depending on the inmate's level of education:

> Class 1 – Secondary Five (Year 11)
> Class 2 – Secondary Three (Year 9)
> Class 3 – Secondary Two (Year 8)
> Class 4 – Secondary One (Year 7)

I'm praying to God that the staff know I'm a second-year university student and will assign me to Class 1. Yesterday I overheard that they might put me in Class 3 for some reason and I panicked. I can't imagine how painful it would be to sit through a bunch of Year 9-level classes morning after morning!

Today, one of my lawyers, Bond Ng, came for a visit. We talked about the pending charges filed against at least four Demosistō core members – myself (contempt of court), Nathan (unlawful assembly), Ivan (unlawful assembly) and Derek (public nuisance). Our calendar is now filled with trials, bail hearings, sentencing, appeals and yet more appeals. The seemingly endless cycle of the criminal justice system keeps me up at night and occupies my mind at every meal. It's surreal that young people like us need to worry about repeatedly being sent to prison, and yet this is the reality that faces us.

Bond and I also discussed the recent typhoon I'd read about in the paper. He told me the winds were so powerful that bricks were seen flying through the air. One of the affected areas was the waterfront along South Horizons where I live with my parents. I really miss my neighbourhood and the people there.

Even though Pik Uk is a relatively civilised prison, it isn't a happy place. Throughout the day there's a lot of yelling – mostly the guards shouting commands at inmates or reprimanding them for something or other – so when Bond shook my hand on his way out, it felt strangely out of place. Since I arrived here, I have not shaken anyone's hand.

I am not treated as an equal by the prison authorities. As a prisoner, I operate in absolute subordination. I must comply with every command without question and address every officer with the honorific 'Sir'. For example, if a guard stops me in my tracks because he wants to speak with me I must put whatever personal belongings I'm carrying – my toothbrush, face towel, books, etc. – on the floor before answering his questions without making direct eye contact.

I read a news story a couple of days ago about Paul Shieh, a respected barrister and former chairman of the Hong Kong Bar Association, who caused an uproar after commenting on a popular radio programme about the recent legal troubles facing political activists. Shieh remarked that Professor Benny Tai and his fellow Occupy Central leaders deserved to go to prison, saying that 'they got what they asked for' when they organised a civil obedience movement. Both Bottle and Bond asked me what I thought of the controversial comment. I told them that the mindset of Shieh and all the other so-called 'social elites' in Hong Kong is what tears our society apart. Call it nepotism or plutocracy, the system always favours the upper rungs and leaves the powerless out in the cold. Just like it does here in Pik Uk.

The most coveted newspaper here is the *Oriental Daily News*. It's pro-Beijing but it has a daily centrefold that's popular among the men. Meanwhile, the only news broadcast on the communal television is from TVB, not a channel I would normally watch. I now appreciate what it's like to be exposed to biased news sources without even realising it. And if nobody realises it, the lemmings will head to the cliff without knowing that there is another way. Luckily for me, because everyone goes straight for the *Oriental Daily*, no one ever touches the shared copy of *Ming Pao*, and every morning my thoughtful cellmate Ah Sun brings it over without me even asking.

Speaking of bias, a prison supervisor approached me this afternoon for a chat over recent news events. He began by declaring himself to be an 'independent', and that he's neither a 'yellow ribbon' (a supporter of the Umbrella Movement) nor a 'blue ribbon' (a supporter of the government and the police). He asked me whether I had any regrets about entering politics and ending up behind bars, before launching into a 30-minute monologue sharing his views on my conviction and the government's appeal against my sentence. His point – if there was one – was similar to what Paul Shieh had said about Professor Tai: we all got what we asked for.

I didn't challenge him, mainly out of self-preservation, but also because I knew nothing I said would ever change his mind. So I just smiled and slowly walked away.

A Six-pronged Plan of Resistance

抵抗威權的六件事

Day 11 – Sunday, 27 August 2017 (Part 1)

Typhoon signal 8 is up. All outdoor activities have been cancelled.

My cellmate and I are cooped up in our 70-square-foot double cell, which gives me plenty of time to compose a longer journal entry. I'm dyslexic – hence the many typos and wrong use of characters – and my handwriting is hopeless. I must apologise in advance to the poor soul who is transcribing my manuscript.

A lot has happened in the past week. From what I read in the paper, last Sunday activists staged a massive street rally – the largest since the Umbrella Movement – in support of Alex, Nathan and me. The huge turnout was largely down to the fact that until recently Hong Kong never had any political prisoners. This new development has rattled a lot of people, especially parents who worry that their children may get locked up too if they participate in politics.

Also this week, Reuters published an exposé suggesting that Justice Secretary Rimsky Yuen had overruled an internal decision not to appeal the sentencing of various convicted activists, including mine. Meanwhile, the Court of Final Appeal refused to hear the appeal filed by two of the six lawmakers who were unseated by Oathgate. And Paul Shieh's callous remarks about Professor Tai receiving his just desserts topped it all off.

Hong Kong is gradually becoming an autocracy. At this critical juncture, pro-democracy activists must reassess the situation and devise a more effective plan of resistance going forward. Here are six ideas for how we can do that.

1. Point out the elephant in the courtroom

Under common law principles, judges are bound by precedents to ensure consistency and fairness. In the case of unlawful assembly, which is a crime under the Public Order Ordinance, the harshest sentence the court has handed out since the Handover is six months (given to anti-government budget protesters who occupied a street in the financial district and clashed with police). Yet the NNT Thirteen are serving sentences ranging from eight to thirteen months. Likewise, Nathan, Alex and myself received six to eight months for our roles in the storming of Civic Square.

In recent judgments, judges have stressed the need to levy heavy sentences as a 'deterrent' against an 'unhealthy trend' of civil unrest. It seems to me that judges are increasingly injecting ideology into their sentencing decisions, as they appear to be more and more willing to use the bench to express their own political views. Although judges are quick to declare political neutrality, the fact that they characterise youth activism as an 'unhealthy' development that ought to be curbed is ample evidence that some judges are anything but neutral.

Even the Public Order Ordinance itself is highly problematic. The law was hastily passed by the Provisional LegCo in Shenzhen, China, during the transitional period following the Handover. The legislative process was shoddy, opaque and involved no public consultation. Disappointingly, judges are now applying and interpreting the ordinance as if it were a robust and ironclad law just like any other. They give no regard to the ordinance's troubled genesis and lack of legitimacy.

Unlawful assembly isn't the only crime in the Public Order Ordinance that the government has used to charge protesters with. Rioting is another frequently used arrow in the ordinance's quiver, and it carries much harsher sentences. Case in point: dozens of protesters in the 2016 Mongkok Chinese New Year civil unrest were charged with rioting. Several of them, including Edward Leung, founder of Hong Kong Indigenous,* received six-year sentences.

In addition to overzealous judges and bad laws, activists have to wrestle with the Department of Justice, which has virtually limitless resources – funded by taxpayers no less – to selectively prosecute individuals long considered a thorn in the government's side. The DOJ appeals court decisions and sentences that aren't to their liking and won't stop until they get the outcome they want. By contrast, few defendants have the financial resources to battle the government in the appellate process and many cut their losses and give up.

Local business elites always rush to defend the city's declining rule of law. They hold up our independent judiciary as a 'bedrock of Hong Kong's

---

* A localist group founded in 2015. More radical than Demosistō, Hong Kong Indigenous advocate a militant approach to civil disobedience. Their political goals include full secession from mainland China.

prosperity' and turn a blind eye to the reality that the criminal justice system is increasingly used as a political tool to silence dissent. They look the other way as one activist after another is sent to prison, as judges hand out sentences that are each longer than the last.

To continue our fight for full democracy, Hong Kongers must wake up to the fact that neither our rule of law nor our independent judiciary is adequate in safeguarding our fundamental rights. The first step to tackling any problem is to admit that there is one: our government has turned the courtroom into an uneven battlefield.

2.   Unite the opposition

Just because we fight for the same cause doesn't mean that we always see eye to eye. Indeed, many within the moderate pan-democratic camp have mis-givings about the approach adopted by more radical groups, such as the NNT Thirteen who stormed a LegCo committee meeting and clashed violently with the police.

Likewise, localist groups are tired of mass marches and slogans. They blame the moderates for the lack of progress despite decades of non-violent campaigns. The result is constant bickering and finger pointing within the opposition, which plays into the hands of the authorities and allows them to divide and conquer.

Differences in tactics notwithstanding, we're all motivated by the same pro-democracy demands. Dozens of activists across the political spectrum have ended up in jail, and many more will do so in the coming months. We must honour them by setting aside our differences and picking up where they left off.

One of the best ways to demonstrate that we can all work together is to set up a fund and solicit donations to provide legal assistance to the accused, regardless of their ideology, and provide counselling and other support to the affected families.

3.   Defend our LegCo foothold

As we continue to take our fight to the streets, we must also make ourselves heard on the legislative floor. The first step to defending our foothold in LegCo is to fill the seats left empty by the six disqualified opposition lawmakers.

At this moment, it's looking increasingly likely that localist candidates (such as those from Hong Kong Indigenous) and candidates who advocate self-determination (such as those from Demosistō) will be barred from running in the by-elections. Earlier this year, Edward Leung was denied his right to run despite having signed a pledge of allegiance to the Basic Law.

Even so, walking away is not an option. Taking a page from the pro-democracy movements in Taiwan and Singapore, we know that giving up on the legislature altogether will only make things worse, not least by allowing the government to pass bad laws with impunity. No matter how unlevel the playing field is, LegCo, like most legislatures around the world, remains an important check and balance on those in power.

As for who should be nominated to fill the six empty seats, I propose two simple selection criteria. First, the candidates must enjoy broad support from the opposition camp and adequately represent the political platforms of the respective lawmakers they are to replace. Second, they must possess the charisma to articulate our political demands and galvanise the public to support our cause.

These by-elections are more than a succession plan; they are a powerful symbol of resistance. Sending pro-democratic representatives back to the legislative chamber will deliver a powerful message to the ruling elites: every legislator they've ousted will be replaced by someone just like him or her.

They can't disqualify us all.

4. Keep faith in non-violent protests

Ever since the Umbrella Movement ended in 2014 without making any tangible political gains, civil society has struggled to cope with the perceived failure. Young people emerging from the movement were left with a deep sense of powerlessness and protest fatigue. Many began to dismiss non-violent protest as a potential means to our political ends.

Meanwhile, activists who advocate for more radical forms of resistance are being crushed under the full force of the law. What happened to the likes of Edward Leung has made young people think twice before hurling another brick at the police.

The pro-democracy movement seems to have stalled. Neither peaceful nor aggressive tactics have brought us closer to where we want to go. Whatever actions we've pursued so far have done little to make our government or Beijing budge.

But isn't that all the more reason for the non-violent camp and the localist groups to join forces? From here on in, let's make every street march a rallying cry to support those who are imprisoned or about to be imprisoned – from non-violence advocates like Professor Tai to use-any-means-necessary localists like Edward Leung. Activists of all stripes have reasons to take to the streets, if not to demand universal suffrage then to express their outrage over political imprisonment, a beast that knows no ideological boundaries.

5.   Cover for the imprisoned

Many supporters have asked me what they can do, aside from writing letters and sharing our news on social media, to help those activists who are behind bars. I always offer the same answer: donate your time.

Other than Alex, Nathan and me, the so-called NNT Thirteen are also doing time in prison. The media call us the '13 plus 3'. To show your solidarity with us, I encourage you to volunteer 16 hours of your time every month – that's one hour for each jailed activist – to do whatever community work speaks to you.

Here are some ideas of what you can do with those 16 hours: hand out political flyers on the streets; man a street stall on a Sunday march; share your views at a community forum; and tell your friends and family to register to vote. You can even join an election campaign for a pro-democracy candidate.

The success of any political movement relies on grassroots efforts at neighbourhood level. Those efforts begin with you. Once I'm out of prison and back on the streets I hope to see you hard at work and making a difference, behind a megaphone or at the front of a crowd.

6.   Be prepared to step up

In the late 1970s, the pro-democracy movement in Taiwan took a bloody, tragic turn. Brutal crackdowns on protesters by the autocratic regime culminated in the so-called 'Formosa Incident'; martial law was declared, protest leaders were arrested, tortured and executed, and many more were tried and given heavy sentences.

Hong Kong has been spared the kind of bloodshed witnessed in Taiwan and neighbouring countries – at least for now. But the price we must pay for demanding political change is expected to rise. Before the 16 of us were sent to prison, we all operated on the assumption that an unlawful assembly conviction would result in no more than a community-service sentence. See how quickly that assumption was disproved.

In Taiwan, after the Formosa Incident a large number of activists were locked up and barred from politics. In response, their spouses, friends and even defence lawyers were called upon to run for election in their place.

Activists in Hong Kong are expected to suffer similar fates in the foreseeable future. Before long, you too may be asked to step up to take their place. When that day comes, I hope you are ready.

Fall In, the Chief Officer is Here

高層殺到, 立正站好

Day 11 – Sunday, 27 August 2017 (Part 2)

Like every other day since I arrived, a handful of inmates and I spent most of today sweeping the 2,000-square-foot canteen. We clean after every breakfast, lunch and dinner.

Most 20-somethings in Hong Kong live with their parents and many middle-class households have a live-in maid. My family is no exception. I've never cleaned this much in my life and I keep telling myself that it's good for my character.

Twice a day, a senior correctional officer visits the facility to ensure that everything is in tip-top shape. All inmates have to stand in a straight line with our chests out, make a fist with both hands, and stare, not straight ahead, but 45 degrees upwards. This last requirement makes no sense to me. I've always assumed that one should make eye contact when addressing a superior, but apparently I've had it all wrong. 'When you look up, you look like you're full of hope,' one of the guards explained.

While we're in position, the senior officer will yell, 'This is an inspection. Any request or complaint?' Of course no one ever says anything except to reply, 'Good morning, Sir!' After that, the officer will say 'Good morning' back, and we'll express our gratitude by answering, 'Thank you, Sir!'

People outside prison, such as my friends and classmates, always call me by my full Chinese name: Wong Chi-fung. It's common in Hong Kong to address friends and acquaintances by their full names and it's not considered overly formal. Here in prison, however, as a friendly gesture of familiarity, staff and inmates alike have shortened my name to 'Fung Jai' (Little Fung), 'Fung Gor' (Brother Fung) or 'Ah Fung' (Fungie).

Everyone at Pik Uk knows who I am. Inmates like to chat with me and discuss prisoners' rights. They all think I can use my 'star power' to make life easier for them. After finishing our chores tonight, a few of us gathered around to complain about some of the ways in which prisons are run in Hong Kong.

One of the biggest gripes is how restrictive 'the list' is. The Correctional Services allow visiting friends and family to bring inmates supplies from the outside, but only if items are on an approved list. This includes basic things like pens, notebooks, razors and face towels. Absent from the list are some basic personal hygiene items like talcum powder and body lotion.

The teenager sitting across from me at the canteen had a more specific request. He complained that Pik Uk doesn't allow 'photo albums' (photo books of nude or semi-nude women), even though other juvenile facilities do. 'We need to fight for equality among prisons!' he joked. 'But, on a more serious note,' he continued, 'I was roughed up pretty badly in the police car after my arrest. Do you think you can push for cameras to be installed in police vehicles?'

Teenager vs Society

少年倉裡的 Teenager

Day 14 – Wednesday, 30 August 2017

I received another large batch of letters today. Some came from Demosistians, some from supporters in Hong Kong and abroad. Other than visits from my parents and friends, the arrival of the mail is the most exciting part of my day.

One letter was from a Hong Konger living in Canada. It brought back memories of a recent trip I took to Toronto with veteran activist Martin Lee, the so-called 'Father of Democracy' and founding chairman of the United Democrats of Hong Kong and the Democratic Party, and Mak Yin-ting, the former chairwoman of the Hong Kong Journalists Association. It feels like a lifetime since I was free to travel around the world and tell our story to parliaments and university students. Those days couldn't be more different from my life here in prison.

I've spent every day of the last two weeks with the same group of inmates. There are about 36 of us – roughly the size of a class at a local secondary school. At the beginning I was pretty guarded around them, partly because some are heavily tattooed street-gang types (the kind your parents would tell you to stay away from), and partly because most of them are here for drug trafficking, robbery, assault or other serious crimes. But once I got to know them, they all seemed genuine and easy to get along with. I realise it was wrong of me to judge them based on their appearance and history.

They all seem to have one thing in common – they like to brag about their pasts. They engage in endless one-upmanship based on the number of runners they used to control in their gangs, the size of their turf, how fiercely they defended and expanded it, things like that. Sometimes the war stories get so OTT and implausible I just roll my eyes and tune them out.

But I do try to understand how they ended up in gangs in the first place. They often share common backgrounds: not getting along with their families, quitting school after Secondary Three (Year 9), and hanging out with 'the wrong crowd'. Listening to them has been eye-opening and humbling. It's completely changed my impression of youth offenders, who are so often portrayed in the mainstream media as vicious and dangerous. In reality they're kids just like me. They spend their days like any average teen, flipping through magazines and burying their noses in books. Many of them are loyal fans of Roy Kwong, a prominent activist, lawmaker and bestselling romance novelist nicknamed 'Kwong God'. When the inmates found out that Nathan and I work closely with Roy, they all wanted to know the secret of how he comes up with such gut-wrenching love stories. I think those questions are best answered by 'the God' himself.

As much as I like Roy and respect his work, I prefer Japanese manga and video games. They are my guilty pleasures. Inmates were surprised when I asked them to lend me *One-Punch Man*, a popular Japanese comic book. I also told them about my obsession with *Gundam*, a timeless Japanese anime series and the country's answer to *Star Trek*. Then it was my turn to brag – I told them I had just bought the new PS4 game console and it was waiting at home to be played.

Sometimes our conversations turn more serious and they'll whine about the local education system. One guy said, 'Kids who do well in school don't end up here. And kids who end up here won't ever do well in school. Nobody ever chooses to be in the second group. The two groups never mix and we may as well live on two different planets.'

His words really made me think. The local education system is notoriously competitive and obsessed with good grades. Lots of kids get pushed out and left behind and once they fall out of the system, no one bothers to try to bring them back. They become one more statistic for the government and scare stories for the media, who write sensation-alist headlines like 'Teens arrested in major drug bust' and 'Gang youth rounded up at underground gambling pit'. When we read the headlines in the newspapers, most of us shake our heads and turn to the next page. We don't expect to hear about these kids ever again. But where have they gone and where can they go?

Just last year, Netflix released *Teenager vs Superpower.* But in the mean streets of Hong Kong, a 'Teenager vs Society' story plays out every day and no one bats an eyelid.

My First March

落場步操

Day 15 – Thursday, 31 August 2017

Today I had my first dreaded morning march. I'm a scrawny, nerdy Hong Kong schoolboy. I spend nearly all my spare time playing video games and watching Japanese anime. I don't go out much and I've never been athletic or particularly coordinated. I'll be lucky to get through the march without embarrassing or hurting myself.

All things considered though, I think I did alright this morning. Other than the few times I turned left when I was supposed to turn right, I held my own just fine. Perhaps years later when I look back on my Pik Uk days I will miss the marches. But for now, my strategy is to lay low in the second row where mistakes are less obvious to the drill sergeant. (In fact, inmates always rush to the main yard at march time to try to call dibs on the second row.)

It was a good start to a jam-packed day. I had several visitors lined up. Lawmakers Charles Mok and Alvin Yeung stopped by before the Legal Aid rep showed up with more paperwork for me to review and sign. After that came my parents, then Lester Shum and lawmaker Eddie Chu.

Before we finished, Eddie looked me in the eye and said, 'Chi-fung, don't think of yourself as being in prison. Think outside these walls.' I knew exactly what he meant. Eddie wanted to remind me that I'm a prisoner of conscience and even though I'm on the other side of the thick glass pane, there are plenty of ways I can make a difference in the outside world.

Eddie's words lifted my spirit and motivated me to think beyond Pik Uk. After all, we live in the age of social media and instant information dissemination. Whatever message I want to deliver to the public, I can say it to my visitors and have them share it on Facebook and Twitter on my behalf.

Speaking of Facebook, I received a letter from Demosistō that contained more than the usual ramblings about party affairs. It had screenshots of Facebook posts that had been shared on my wall from friends and colleagues. It was surreal to go through social media on printed paper instead of a smartphone. But it hit the spot and eased my Facebook withdrawal symptoms, however temporarily.

On an unrelated note, there's no shortage of propaganda in youth prison. Every classroom, computer room and common area is plastered with posters featuring slogans like 'Knowledge can change your destiny' and 'Reform for a better tomorrow'. Every prison poster bears the same butterfly motif. I asked one of the guards what it symbolised. Beaming with pride he told me that butterflies represent transformation. He explained that youth offenders are like caterpillars that will morph into beautiful butterflies by the end of their sentences – but only if they are willing to be rehabilitated. If they follow the programme of the Correctional Services they will spread their wings and take flight once they reintegrate into society.

I wonder how many inmates register the metaphor.

Letters from the Heart

有信有心

Day 16 – Friday, 1 September 2017

I received 40 letters today – a new record for me. The senders came from all walks of life, including university students and professors, a *Wall Street Journal* reporter, a Hong Kong expatriate living in Australia and a young mother who gave birth to her son in 2014 at the height of the mass protests. She calls him her 'umbrella baby'.

I really enjoy reading the personal anecdotes my supporters share with me. One mother wrote that she had asked her son to draw me a picture of the Transformers to cheer me up, only to discover in embarrassment that she had mixed up *Transformers* and *Gundam*, the anime I like. A father talked about taking his family of five to a street rally for the first time, and how jam-packed the metro station was on that day. A self-professed 'politically apathetic middle-class citizen' confessed how he used to think TVB News was the reigning authority in news reporting until the Umbrella Movement inspired him to be more critical and take mainstream local media with a pinch of salt. A Facebook follower urged me to hang on to my imaginary 'crest of courage' (an amulet from the *Digimon* anime) and a particularly thoughtful supporter printed a copy of my mother's open letter to Chief Executive Carrie Lam, which was published on the online news portal *HK01* and urged Lam to start listening to young people, instead of trying to silence them by using the criminal justice system.

These letters are evidence of the Umbrella Movement's greatest achievement: political awakening. Even though the phrase has been overused to the point that it has lost much of its meaning, no one can deny or question the fact that the movement has jolted a generation of Hong Kong citizens out of their existential coma and political apathy. Had it not been for those 79 days of mass protests in 2014, no one would have bothered to pick up a pen and craft a letter to a 20-year-old behind bars. The outpouring of support shown to me and other jailed activists is proof that a seed has been planted in the mind of every freedom-loving Hong Konger, ready to sprout when the conditions are ripe.

These letters also answer a recurrent question many have asked me: after all that Hong Kongers went through in 2014, and given how helpless and hopeless everyone has felt since, how do I, a leading activist, plan to energise the public to fight alongside me?

My answer is this: the only way to galvanise society is to make real sacrifices and put our money where our mouth is. Bearing the cross of imprisonment as the '13 plus 3' activists have done is the best way to prove our commitment to Hong Kong and demonstrate that we are more than mere slogans and rhetoric. The heartfelt letters that keep coming are proof that our efforts haven't gone unnoticed.

Counting the Days

數數日子

Day 18 – Sunday, 3 September 2017 (Part 1)

There are no classes or chores on Sundays. It's the only day of the week that inmates are allowed to wear open-toed sandals. These rubber sandals have come to symbolise idleness for me.

This morning we were given a couple of hours of free time to do our own thing in the canteen. In the afternoon, we were given yet more hours to fill in the classroom. Most inmates chose to watch television, which is pretty much the only form of entertainment in youth prison. Some half-heartedly picked up a newspaper or a book to read.

During a very slow conversation, one inmate told me that if my release date happens to fall on a Sunday or public holiday they'll release me a day early. That little prison titbit prompted me to immediately check the dog tag I have to wear around my neck where my release date is marked. My projected release date – 17 December, assuming good behaviour – is indeed on a Sunday! The idea that I'd just 'saved' one day sent me all the way to cloud nine. But I'd barely wiped the smile off my face when I realised it might be too good to be true. The other contempt of court charge I'm facing will likely delay my release date by weeks, if not months.

My contempt hearing is still scheduled for mid-September. Assuming I plead guilty (which my lawyer has recommended), I'll likely get a three-month sentence, which, assuming I get a third off for good behaviour means a net jail time of two months. That makes 16 February my actual release date. I checked again and found, to my delight, that 16 February is Chinese New Year, a statutory holiday. So it looks like I'll benefit from the one-day discount after all.

But even with that, the idea of not being able to spend Chinese New Year's Eve – akin to Thanksgiving or Christmas elsewhere in the world – with my family has once again tempered my excitement.

Checking the calendar, 16 February is 166 days away. That's less than 24 weeks – 6 more in the youth prison and 18 in the adult ward. It makes me feel a bit better to measure time in weeks and break it up into two chunks: before and after my 21st birthday.

I had no visitors today, which made the day feel even longer. My only solace was reading a letter Alex wrote from prison that appeared in the *Apple Daily*, as well as the delivery of the post at 4pm.

In Alex's article he echoed the same sentiment that other jailed activists feel, or are at least supposed to feel: that those in power can imprison our bodies, but they can't imprison our minds. I must admit that Alex's mantra is more easily said than done. The first things I think about when I wake up are my parents and my friends.

Equally torturous is seeing advertisements for all the food I can't eat on the TV and in newspapers. Sometimes prison food is so bland that I can only finish half of it and go to bed hungry. What would I give to have a sip of coffee or a coke? Or a bite of sushi, a steak or wonton noodles.

An Open Letter to the International Community

寫給國際社會的信

Day 18 – Sunday, 3 September 2017 (Part 2)

To friends abroad who care about Hong Kong:

It's been a month since I arrived in Pik Uk. Even though I'm behind bars, I can still feel the outpouring of support from the international community, in particular from human rights organisations around the world and lawmakers in the United Kingdom, the United States and Germany. All of you have expressed concern and outrage over the imprisonment of the '13 plus 3'. We are eternally indebted to you.

Three years ago, I joined hundreds of thousands of brave citizens in the largest political movement in Hong Kong's history with the simple and honourable goal to bring true democracy to our city. We asked to exercise our constitutional right to elect our own leader through a fair and open election.

Not only did the Hong Kong government – appointed by Beijing and under its direction – ignore our demands, it also arrested and charged many of us with illegal assembly. Including me. After a lengthy trial and taking into account our unselfish motivations and generally accepted principles of civil disobedience, the lower court sentenced us to community service.

Then things took an ominous turn. An investigative report by Reuters revealed that our Secretary of Justice Rimsky Yuen, an appointee of our unelected Chief Executive Carrie Lam, overruled the community-service order recommended by his prosecution committee and made a politically motivated decision to appeal my sentence. The appeal was heard by a High Court judge who had been photographed at events hosted by pro-Beijing organisations. Ultimately, the judge increased my sentence to six months in prison on the grounds that the court needed to put a stop to the 'troubling trend' of political activism.

Until recently, the charge of unlawful assembly was used only to prosecute members of local gangs. Now, I believe the real 'troubling trend' is that a counter-organised crime tool is being deployed to silence dissenters and snuff out the pro-democracy movement in Hong Kong. Until recently, participants in civil disobedience efforts had always been handed community-service orders. The prison sentences received by the '13 plus 3' represent yet another 'troubling trend' that has significantly increased the price of political activism in Hong Kong.

Tomorrow, Professor Benny Tai, Professor Chan Kin-man and Reverend Chu Yiu-ming will likely go to prison for their roles in Occupy Central, the civil disobedience campaign that led to the Umbrella Movement. Their imprisonment is yet more evidence that freedom of assembly and other fundamental rights in Hong Kong are being eroded at a quickening pace.

In the past, the term 'political prisoner' conjured up frightening images of dissidents in mainland China being rounded up and thrown into jail. It's hard to imagine that the term now also applies to Hong Kong, one of the world's freest economies. As Beijing's long arm reaches into every corner of Hong Kong and threatens our freedoms and way of life, the number of prisoners of conscience is only going to increase. The international community can no longer stand on the sidelines and pretend that it is business as usual in Hong Kong. Something needs to be done.

Unfortunately, few foreign governments are willing to take on the world's second largest economy and hold its actions to account. For instance, I was disheartened by the latest 'Six-Monthly Report on Hong Kong' published by the British Secretary of State for Foreign and Commonwealth Affairs Boris Johnson.* Despite the political persecution of activists like myself, the Foreign Secretary concluded that the 'one country, two systems' framework was 'working well'. As a signatory to the Sino-British Joint Declaration on Hong Kong, Britain has both a moral and a legal obligation to defend its former subjects and speak up on their behalf.

I hasten to add that there are many individuals and organisations in the West that have steadfastly supported the pro-democracy movement in Hong Kong. With his remark that our names will be 'carved into history', Chris Patten has been a great source of encouragement to me, Nathan and Alex. A *New York Times* editor has even suggested that the three of us be nominated for the Nobel Peace Prize.† Their words humble us. What should be carved into history is the Umbrella Movement that awakened a generation of Hong Kong's youth. The ones who deserve a Nobel are every Hong Konger

---

* Appointed Prime Minister of the United Kingdom in 2019.
† In February 2018, Joshua Wong, Nathan Law and Alex Chow were nominated for the Nobel Peace Prize. At 21 years old, Joshua was the youngest of the three. They were Hong Kong's first ever nominees for the prize.

who stood bravely in the face of an intransigent regime backed by an authoritarian superpower.

Compared to the 1.4 billion people in mainland China – that's nearly one in five people on this planet – the population of 7 million in Hong Kong is infinitesimal. But what we lack in numbers, we make up for in determination and grit. Every day we are guided by our thirst for freedom and a sense of duty to bring democracy to our children and grandchildren. So long as we follow that path, we will always be on the right side of history.

The island of Hong Kong may be small, but the resolve of its people is anything but.

This Time Last Year I Was Counting Votes at LegCo

一年前還在立法會點票站

Day 19 – Monday, 4 September 2017

Today's mail delivery broke another personal record, not by the number of letters but by its sheer weight. From my lawyer I received a 291-page printout of my entire Facebook page and Demosistō's group page since my sentencing two weeks ago.

I never thought I would enjoy this 'hardcopy Facebook' – almost a contradiction in terms – but I do. It makes me feel connected with the outside world again. I've thought about requesting regular Facebook printouts but decided against it. For one thing, the task is time-consuming (Demosistians are already time-poor and short of hands) and for another, printing reams and reams of Facebook posts would kill far too many trees. I'll just have to wait for the occasional surprise, like today's.

Every letter coming in and going out of prison will be opened and reviewed by the guards, on the grounds that Correctional Services need to check for hidden objects. They also screen for unauthorised messages, like plans to subvert the authorities or conspiracy among inmates.

Unless, that is, the letter is to or from a person who holds a public office, such as a legislator. If this is the case, the envelope will remain unopened and unread by anyone other than the addressee. Delivery is also expedited so it takes two days instead of a full week to get to the hands of the recipient. The sender doesn't even need to put a postage stamp on the envelope.

This creates a bit of a loophole and one that I'm happy to exploit. It saves me stamp money and gives me peace of mind when discussing sensitive matters. The guards grumble each time I request a so-called 'sealed delivery'. Whether they like it or not, I'm determined to send one at least twice a week.

All sealed deliveries go through the Reception Office. To avoid inmates smuggling drugs or other illegal substances we're required to take a urine test after each sealed delivery pick-up or drop-off. The Reception Office is a glorified locker room where simple paperwork is processed and prison officers sit around and gossip. While waiting in the office to take a drug test one time, my eyes were drawn to the calendar pinned on the wall. Exactly a year ago, on 4 September 2016, Nathan made history by becoming the youngest elected lawmaker in Asia, having won 50,818 votes in the Hong Kong Island constituency. All of us were in the ballot room at the LegCo Building cheering and crying tears of joy, a throng of local and foreign reporters waiting impatiently outside. None of us would have guessed that months after the historic win, Nathan would lose his seat and both of us would be behind bars.

I wonder if Nathan, too, has noticed the anniversary, and I wonder what's going through his mind tonight.

Bland and Blander

重複單調乏味的食物

Day 20 – Tuesday, 5 September 2017

From the day I started keeping a journal, I've expected friends and family to take great interest in what kind of food I've been eating in prison. And so I've made it a point to jot down what I ate every day at breakfast, lunch and dinner.

Day	Breakfast	Lunch	Dinner	Night snack
Mon	pork cucumbers	sweet porridge buttered bread	chicken wing vegetables	raisin roll milk
Tue	beef vegetables	savoury porridge jam and bread	fish, egg vegetables	raisin roll milk
Wed	chicken wing cucumbers	sweet porridge buttered bread	fish vegetables	raisin roll milk
Thurs	pork vegetables	savoury porridge jam and bread	chicken wing vegetables	raisin roll milk
Fri	beef cucumbers	sweet porridge buttered bread	fish, egg vegetables	raisin roll milk

Day	Breakfast	Lunch	Dinner	Night snack
Sat	chicken wing vegetables	savoury porridge jam and bread	fish vegetables	raisin roll milk
Sun	beef balls cucumbers milk tea	tofu skin porridge buttered roll	fish, egg vegetables	raisin roll milk

I stopped recording my diet after about two weeks, when I realised the menu repeats itself week after week and never changes.

An 'Ill-mannered' Speech

「不懂大體」的一番話

Day 22 – Thursday, 7 September 2017

The headline of every newspaper today relates to the government's proposed national anthem law.

Yesterday, Beijing published a draft bill to criminalise the commercial use or parodies of the Chinese national anthem, 'The March of the Volunteers'. Anyone caught 'intentionally insulting' the anthem could face up to three years in prison.

The bill is another encroachment on our freedom of expression. Like the national education curriculum that Scholarism thwarted in 2012, it's the latest attempt by the government to legislate patriotism. It didn't work in 2012 and it won't work today.

Sadly, LegCo is dominated by Beijing loyalists (especially after Oathgate's recent purge of pro-democracy lawmakers) and the government has more than enough votes to pass the bill as soon as the public consultation period ends.

Several newspapers reported a student's speech that has turned heads and earned widespread praise. At the opening ceremony of her secondary school, Tiffany Tong, the school's 17-year-old student union president, weighed in on the national anthem debate when she addressed the student body:

> The way young people choose to express their grievances about their government, such as turning their backs to the national flag, is often considered ill-mannered and disrespectful.
>
> Yes, we know that manners are important – we're taught that every day in school – but we also know the importance of our principles and beliefs.
>
> In the eyes of many adults we're rude, disobedient and unpragmatic. But we are doing what young people are supposed to do: challenge conventional wisdom and refuse to compromise. Along the way we are bound to make mistakes and stumble, but we'll emerge from our mistakes and stumbles as stronger and better people.

Tiffany's words are prodigious. They perfectly sum up the collective sentiment of the next generation in

Hong Kong. Facing ever-growing social injustices and political bullying by Communist China, young people refuse to give in and trade their ideals for what's easy and pragmatic. Instead of hunkering down and living a 'well-mannered' life, the way adults do, they are choosing to risk it all by speaking up and pushing back.

I was enormously encouraged by what I read. When we disbanded Scholarism to make way for Demosistō, some members worried that we might lose an important platform to inspire the next generation of teenage activists. Tiffany is proof that we need not worry.

The Flexible Politician

靈活的政治家

Day 24 – Saturday, 9 September 2017

A trio of Demosistians came to see me today. The main subject of conversation was the upcoming LegCo by-elections. As the nomination deadline approaches, there's some urgency for us to agree on which one of us should run. The answer depends on who we're running against.

Our main opponent is Judy Chan from the pro-establishment New People's Party (NPP). Chan was educated in Australia and worked in the US before returning to Hong Kong to enter politics. In a recent interview, Chan said her husband was against her decision to run for LegCo, not only because he was concerned about the stress an election campaign could bring, but also because she would be obliged to give up her American citizenship and in doing so, potentially make it harder for her daughter to attend a US university in the future.

The NPP is a party of business elites. Its members come from the upper crust of Hong Kong society, who cosy up to the Communist Party with their patriotic rhetoric while holding onto the foreign passports that are their potential escape route. They own luxury property abroad and send their children to universities in the West to shield them from the local education system. It makes it all the more ironic that Beijing accuses leaders of the Umbrella Movement and pro-democracy activists of acting under the influence of 'foreign powers'. Their own so-called loyalists have more foreign ties than any of us.

During a district by-election in 2014, Chan lambasted the outgoing district councilman – a pro-democracy politician – for abandoning his local constituencies to run for LegCo. She told voters she would focus on district affairs and that she had no ambition to become a lawmaker. She ended up winning the election.

Two years later, after Oathgate created an opening for her, Chan has no qualms about going back on her word and throwing her hat into the ring. I wonder what her constituencies make of that?

My Chinese-made Radio

國產收音機
_____

Day 25 – Sunday, 10 September 2017

Two weeks ago I spent some of my hard-earned money on an FM radio.

My order arrived today. I've been looking forward to an RTHK* phone-in current affairs programme called *Open Line, Open View* and I was really excited to open the box. I was expecting the same Sony model that other inmates have purchased recently using the provision order form. But it turned out to be a Chinese knock-off. (Later on I found out that Sony have recently stopped manufacturing radios.) A Chinese brand would be fine if it worked, but when I turn on the unit in my cell I hear nothing but static. I get some reception if I stretch my arm through the iron bars of my door

_____

* Radio Television Hong Kong public broadcaster.

and place the unit as far out as possible, but that's no way to listen to the radio.

So I put away my useless radio and opened my mail. One of the letters was from Senia Ng, a young barrister whose father was a cofounder of the Democratic Party, Hong Kong's oldest political party. She enclosed over 50 pages of articles relating to the National Anthem Bill, writings by Alex from prison and even a few sudoku and jumble puzzles.

On the subject of games, earlier today I played ping-pong with some inmates in the common room. We play a few times a week. I'm terrible at sports and never enjoyed them at school, but I managed to hold my own with the table-tennis paddle. I've never exercised as much in my life. My mum must be so proud!

How Much Did They Pay You?

其實你有無錢收?

_____

Day 27 – Tuesday, 12 September 2017

Reading makes the day go by faster. My parents try to bring me new books every time they visit and friends send me reading lists.

I've just finished reading *The Protester* by mainland dissident writer Xu Zhiyuan and the three-volume *One Hundred Years of Pursuit: The Story of Taiwan's Democratic Movement* by Cui-lian Chen, Wu Nai-teh and Hu Hui-ling. I'm looking forward to reading *How Do We Change Our Society?* by sociologist Eiji Oguma, a book given to me as a present by two young Japanese professors via Agnes, who visited Tokyo earlier this year.

Most inmates read whatever is available in the library – tabloid magazines, romance novels and comic books. I try not to walk around with my serious, dense non-fiction on display. I'd enjoy leafing through cooking magazines if they didn't make me crave proper food even more. Japanese *One-Punch Man* manga comes in handy as a guilty pleasure that also helps me blend in with others.

For the past five years I've been moving in circles with politicians and activists. We sometimes live in a bubble, saying and doing things that make us look out of touch with the general population. I'm making a conscious effort to connect with my fellow inmates. Listening to them vent about what they've been through has broadened my horizons and brought me back down to earth.

More than one inmate has asked me, 'How much do they pay you to do your political stuff?' At first I thought they just wanted to provoke me with accusations that I take money from foreign governments. But I've slowly realised the questions are genuine. Most people don't understand why any sane person would risk prison to do what I do if it wasn't for money. So now I just smile and say, 'I wish I did get paid!' But no one ever believes me. I've thought about saying that I'm just like someone who volunteers their time to help others without expecting anything in return. What I really want to tell them, but don't for fear of sounding self-righteous, is that my sole purpose for entering politics is to make a difference. I do it so that I can one day tell my children and grandchildren that I've given something for the city they love. That would be worth all the money in the world.

Boredom Busters

解悶工廠

Day 28 – Wednesday, 13 September 2017

FronTiers is a group of social workers, lawyers and reporters who came together to support activists in need. Together with lawmaker Eddie Chu, the group started a letter-writing campaign called 'Boredom Busters', collecting letters and reading materials to help the '13 plus 3' fight the most formidable enemy in prison: time.

I got my first FronTiers package today – a 30-page document with newspaper clippings and printouts of online articles. Even though I make a habit of reading the *Apple Daily* every morning, some of the best political analysis and reports are only available through independent online news outlets that cover small but significant news events often overlooked by the broadsheets.

Reading a stack of computer printouts may not be everyone's idea of having a good time, but there I was, flipping the crisp pages in the canteen and feeling the warmth of every Boredom Busters' volunteer who had taken the time to make my prison sentence go by just that little bit faster.

I saw in the news clippings that my sentence appeal is now public knowledge. Some of the articles mentioned that I would be out on bail by early October. What they didn't mention was the likelihood of that happening. So far my lawyers have been trying to manage my expectations. They estimate that my chance of being granted bail by October is less than 50–50. For now, I'll continue to be what politicians call 'cautiously optimistic'.

Do You See Those Skyscrapers?

你看那到些高樓嗎?

Day 30 – Friday, 15 September 2017

I received another hefty mail delivery today. I noticed that most of the letters were dated more than a week ago and it made me wonder why my mail is taking longer and longer to reach me. I don't think I'll ever find out the reason why.

Two things I read in the morning kept churning around in my head all day.

The first is an article by *Initium* reporter Vivian Tam. I've known Vivian since my anti-national education campaign in 2012. Five years on, her pen is as sharp as ever. In her article for the digital media outlet, 'Safeguarding the truth and protecting our history', she charts the evolution of Hong Kong's pro-democracy movement and compares the Umbrella Movement to similar transformative events in Asia such as the 228 Massacre in Taiwan* and the Gwangju Uprising in South Korea.† Both were bloody popular uprisings that eventually led to the democratisation of the entire countries.

Despite the geographical proximity of Taiwan and South Korea, and that they are two of the most popular travel destinations for Hong Kongers, most of us know very little about their histories and how they came to be the modern democracies they are today. I admit I'm not as well versed in their histories as I should be and I've made a note to ask my family to send me a few books about them.

The other thought-provoking article was from a new columnist who goes by the pen name Ha Mook Mook. In her article 'Forgive me for leaving Hong Kong', she remembers the first night of the

---

* An anti-government uprising in 1947 that was violently suppressed by Taiwan's National Revolutionary Army on behalf of the ruling government. Thousands of citizens were killed and many more injured and imprisoned. The event marked the beginning of the White Terror, a 38-year period of martial law during which tens of thousands of Taiwanese were imprisoned, disappeared or died.

† A popular uprising in South Korea that took place in May 1980 in response to the violent suppression of local students who were demonstrating against martial law. Over 600 people, mostly students, were killed.

Umbrella Movement, and describes her conflicted emotions when she saw entire highways occupied by pro-democracy protesters:

> I know Hong Kong isn't perfect. It has its fair share of social injustices and urban maladies. Sometimes just getting through the day can be tough. But no matter how often I get lost in the dizzying streets and the soaring sky-scrapers, I never cease to be amazed by the beauty of this place.
>
> Everywhere I look tonight, I see courage, imagination and hope – things that I've never seen in the two decades that I've lived here. Hong Kong, you are beautiful!
>
> I won't lie to you – I'm worried that your beauty may not last. I need to hurry and cap-ture these images on film, before the colourful wall is washed out, the tents are taken down, the traffic returns and the people disappear. Before strangers no longer say hello to each other on the streets.
>
> On an anonymous stretch of the highway, a man says to me, 'Can you see the skyscrap-ers over there? That's not the real Hong Kong. Now can you see the crowds down here? That's the real Hong Kong.'

Inmate Abuse

囚犯被打

Day 32 – Sunday, 17 September 2017

Not much happens on Sundays. We spend much of our day off sitting around and chatting, or 'blowing water' as we say in Cantonese. We don't usually have a specific topic, although I've tried to steer the conversation to inmate abuse so that I can pass on any useful information to Bottle. I made a promise to him and I want to honour it. It's a sensitive subject and it didn't take long for the prison guards to catch on – they snoop around and listen in on our discussions – but, whatever the authorities think, I've taken on this issue and I'm not about to drop it for fear of reprisal.

Despite the outright denial by the Correctional Services' Rehabilitation Unit, the division in charge of prisoners' welfare, and the defensive attitude of pretty much every person of authority that Bottle has spoken to, prison violence is so prevalent in Hong Kong that it can be called an epidemic. Bottle also told me that out of the thousands of complaints filed over the past decade, only a handful of cases have been accepted and validated by the Complaints Investigation Unit. It's hardly surprising considering that the head of the unit is appointed by none other than the Commissioner of Correctional Services. There's little, if any, accountability in the system.

It's one thing to look at this issue of inmate abuse in the abstract, quite another to hear first-hand accounts of physical – and sometimes sexual – violence from victims sitting right in front of me. Many of the stories are harrowing. Some have been groped in the groin, others force-fed water mixed with cigarette ash, while some have been made to beat their own hands with wooden clubs until their fingers are broken.

I know that many inmates still believe politics has nothing to do with them and that they have nothing to do with it. That's why they struggle to understand why anyone would enter into politics if not for financial gains. Each time the topic comes up, I tell them that politics is all around them and that it affects every aspect of their lives, from the cigarette tax they pay to the minimum wage they will one day take home and the monthly rent that absorbs almost all of their parents' income. They needn't even look beyond the prison walls to see its effects. Politics is why so many inmates are abused and so few officers are held to account. 'Do you still think politics has nothing to do with you?' I ask.

Hair Politics – Part 1

髮政一

Day 33 – Monday, 18 September 2017

Other than prison abuse, head shaving is another institutional injustice that drives me insane.

At Pik Uk all male juvenile inmates are subject to a mandatory biweekly head shave, without exception. Our hair must be kept shorter than the arbitrary maximum length of 6 millimetres. Twice a month, 40 or so of us are turned into Buddhist monks against our will.

It reminds me of a constitutional challenge lodged by lawmaker Leung Kwok-hung three years ago. Nicknamed 'Long Hair' for his trademark shoulder-length locks, Leung was one of the six who lost their LegCo seats in Oathgate. Just before the Umbrella Movement erupted, he was jailed for forcibly entering a political event. Alleging gender discrimination, Leung took the government to court for cutting his hair in prison while female inmates are allowed to keep theirs long. The Court of First Instance, the lower court of the High Court, below the Court of Appeal, ruled in Leung's favour, but the case is currently pending an appeal.*

I understand that prisoners shouldn't expect to enjoy the same rights as ordinary citizens, and I appreciate that keeping inmates' hair short serves a practical purpose, such as eradicating hair lice. Nevertheless, there's no reason why Pik Uk needs to impose such a strict requirement when other facilities don't. I fail to see any security or health threat posed by male inmates sporting, say, a standard schoolboy haircut.

What upsets me even more is what happened when I suggested to prison management that the matter be brought to the attention of the Justice of the Peace in charge of prison affairs on his next visit. They responded with anger and threats; Sergeant Wong, who is responsible for my ward, warned, 'If you try to talk even one inmate into taking this issue any further I can charge you with incitement to disrupt prison order.'

----

* In January 2019 the Court of Appeal refused to hear Leung's appeal on the grounds that his case 'does not involve questions of great general or public importance'.

Sargeant Wong's response left me dumbfounded and angry. It revealed the authorities' utter disregard for prisoners' welfare. Expressing my concerns about head-shaving to a Justice of the Peace is well within my rights and precisely the kind of concern that is the purpose of his visits. What's more, if this is the level of intimidation levelled at someone like me, a public figure protected to some extent by the glare of the media, then I can't imagine what a regular inmate with no political connections would suffer. No wonder so many inmates choose to keep their mouths shut, irrespective of the injustices.

On a happier note, I received two-dozen letters today, many of them from friends and colleagues overseas. I was especially delighted to hear from Anna Cheung, founder of the New Yorkers Supporting Hong Kong group (NY4HK), who has worked tirelessly for years to help pro-democracy politicians such as Martin Lee and Anson Chan, who created the Hong Kong 2020 group to monitor progress towards constitutional reform by 2020, meet influential politicians in the West. Since the Umbrella Movement Anna has been instrumental in Demosistō's efforts to lobby support from the international community.

I also heard from Jobie Yip, a Hong Kong student at the London School of Economics, who I befriended after giving a talk at Oxford University in 2015. Jobie was one of the overseas students who protested outside the Chinese embassy in London during the Umbrella Movement and the first person to join Demosistō after Nathan's disqualification from LegCo earlier this year. It was a bold decision, considering that Oathgate has effectively barred anyone in the self-determination camp from future elections. If she has any political ambition her affiliation with Demosistō is pretty much a political career-ending move.

Committed overseas Hong Kongers such as Anna and Jobie are critical partners in our fight for democracy. Even though they are far away geographically, their hearts are with us and their solidarity has been one of the major engines behind the push to raise international awareness about the political situation in Hong Kong. What's more, they are a testament to the indelible impact of the Umbrella Movement, which is felt not only in Hong Kong but everywhere else in the world where Hong Kong people can be seen and heard.

Messages from friends are a morale booster, but mail from total strangers often packs the greatest emotional punch. I received a letter from a 14-year-old girl today, who wrote in beautiful handwriting about the way recent political events have made her feel. I don't often receive letters from secondary school students (pen and paper seem anachronistic in the age of WhatsApp and Telegram) and she clearly took a lot of effort and time to craft hers. It's always a treat to hear from people who are the same age I was when I first started my journey in political activism.

Another heartfelt letter came from a young mother, whose last paragraph moved me to tears:

> My baby girl was barely a year old when my husband and I brought her with us to one of your anti-national education demonstrations. We spent the entire evening in Admiralty, hoping that she would soak up the energy at the protest site and grow up to be as brave and stubbornly principled as you.
>
> That was five years ago and she is almost six now. To our surprise, she still remembers that night in Admiralty like it was last week. Each time we drive through the area, she'll point at the section of the highway where we sat for hours. She calls you 'Brother Admiralty' whenever she sees you in the news.
>
> Last week I asked her whether she wanted to do something to support 'Brother

Admiralty', who has been thrown into jail for doing what he believes to be just. I suggested that she draw you some pictures, since she loves to draw. And so here you are, three drawings from the little sister you've never met.

Hair Politics – Part 2

髮政二

___

Day 34 – Tuesday, 19 September 2017

I read in the paper today that the 26-year-old activist Sulu Sou became the youngest lawmaker in Macau in Sunday's general election.

Macau is a former Portuguese colony that, like Hong Kong, reverted to Chinese rule and became a special administrative region before the turn of the millennium. Best known for its mega-casinos, Macau too has been fighting for a free vote and battling the dual evils of corporatocracy and political cronyism. With a population of less than 700,000 (one-tenth of Hong Kong's), the city lacks the critical mass of experienced politicians for a meaningful pro-democracy movement to take hold.

But in 2014, the same year that Taiwan had its

Sunflower Revolution* and Hong Kong witnessed the Umbrella Movement, Macanese citizens exercised their civic power and said 'enough is enough' to political injustices. In May that year, 20,000 protesters took to the streets to oppose a government proposal to enrich the ruling elites with generous retirement packages. The government eventually withdrew the controversial plan and the incident was considered the biggest victory for civil society in Macau's post-handover history. Riding on the surge in political awareness, Sulu managed to make a name for himself and gain mainstream acceptance.

His election win this week is hugely encouraging for all of us, but I also feel a twinge of sadness. Sulu's success story reminds me of Nathan's dramatic political rise and fall – and of the way the youngest lawmaker of Hong Kong won and lost his LegCo seat within just eight months.

Meanwhile, there have been some developments on the head-shaving front. Pik Uk authorities granted me an audience with senior management

---

* The occupation of the Taiwanese legislature by a coalition of students protesting against a proposed bilateral agreement with China (the Cross-Strait Service Trade Agreement, or CSSTA).

this morning. At the meeting, representatives tried to justify the practice by citing hygiene and health concerns, such as excessive perspiration during the summer months.

When I pressed them about the 6-millimetre limit, they conceded that there are no hard and fast rules in the written guidelines and that the length was agreed among officials simply out of 'operational efficiency'. They said they would reach out to other juvenile facilities to establish what best practice would be.

I responded to the representatives blankly. 'The fact that you need to check with other prisons means that Pik Uk doesn't have a specific length requirement beyond the general principle of keeping our hair short. In other words, the 6-millimetre maximum is a made-up rule that I believe you should stop imposing on us.' The men looked at each other and declared the meeting over.

Losing My Cellmate

失去囚友

Day 35 – Wednesday, 20 September 2017

Every three months or so there's an inmate reshuffle at Pik Uk and cellmates are reassigned. The idea is that newcomers can be paired with more experienced inmates who will show them the ropes, while any cliques or potentially dangerous alliances can be broken up.

In this round of cell moves, not only did I lose the cellmate I've grown to like over the past five weeks – I wasn't assigned a new cellmate at all. Prison management probably sees me as too much of a troublemaker to be paired with a new cellmate without infecting his mind. Either that or they think I won't be much of a mentor when it comes to prison duties.

At first I thought it would be a treat to have all 70 square feet to myself, after all, in Hong Kong you'd have to pay an arm and a leg to get that kind of space. But after spending the first night alone, I've realised how isolated I feel without someone to talk to at night. In the coming weeks, I'll have to get used to coming back to an empty cell after dinner – it's the eternal question of privacy vs companionship.

I remember meeting Ah Sun for the first time, 35 days ago. We didn't have much in common and neither of us was too eager to engage with the other. I was raised a Christian in a middle-class family and went to a Direct Subsidy Scheme school (private schools subsidised by the government that are considered better quality than government-run public schools). Ah Sun, like most other inmates, comes from a broken home, dropped out of secondary school and joined a local gang. When he sat down to talk in our cell I couldn't understand half of his gang speak; I would hide in a corner reading a newspaper.

But over time I picked up more and more jargon and began to understand Ah Sun better. I learned to stop dropping English words into my Cantonese to sound less elitist and pompous. Now we sit around and talk as if we were in the same gang.

Most importantly, I really got to know Ah Sun, and I'm proud to call him my friend.

Interrogation by the Security Unit

保安組問話

Day 38 – Saturday, 23 September 2017

I found out today that several inmates I often eat with have been interrogated by prison authorities. After we finished today's physical check-up, about 12 of them were escorted away by the security unit. They were taken to a room, asked to divulge the details of our conversations and warned that mixing with me might get them sent to solitary confinement.

The security unit must have gone through the canteen's CCTV recordings to identify the people they wanted to question. In truth, we rarely discuss prison affairs openly – most of the time we chat about random things like video games, exam strategies and career options. But management is paranoid that my head-shaving campaign might get out of hand and lead to an all-out prison rebellion if it's not contained. The incident echoes the unpleasant conversation I had with Sergeant Wong a few days ago when he threatened me with incitement charges if I were to involve other inmates in my prison activism. It also brings home the reality of living under 24-hour surveillance, watched over by Big Brother at all times and in all places.

Knowing that the visitation area is also closely monitored, I haven't mentioned anything to my visitors about the threats and the interrogation. Instead we talk about recent news events and campaign strategies for the by-elections.

Alone in my empty cell, I reflected on what happened at Pik Uk this past week. I realised that my vocal advocacy for prisoners' rights may have put others inmates in jeopardy. Thinking more broadly, perhaps every political movement I've either led or participated in over the past five years has had the same impact on my loved ones. I've always operated on the assumption that I'm prepared to pay whatever price it takes to fight for my beliefs, but have I once paused to think about my family and consider the tremendous pressure that my actions, no matter how noble in my own mind, have created? Have I once sought their consent, or have I simply taken their understanding for granted?

Watching *Hong Kong Connection*

看的《鏗鏘集》

Day 40 – Monday, 25 September 2017

Hong Kong Connection, one of the longest running current affairs shows in Hong Kong, airs every Monday night at 6pm.

This week's episode was all about activists in prison. I was excited to see several Demosistians being interviewed, including Derek Lam, Isaac Cheng and Jobie Yip. They were filmed opening letters from supporters addressed to Nathan and me. Seeing them chatting and working away on the small screen made me miss them even more.

Most of the scenes were shot in our new office, which is markedly smaller than the workspace we used to have before Nathan lost his seat. After Oathgate, we were evicted from the LegCo Building and had to scramble to find an affordable office space.

Towards the end of the 30-minute episode, Derek said:

> It's been six years since Chi-fung and I entered politics – we've gone from Secondary Four to our third year at university. We became activists because we wanted to make Hong Kong a better place. But has it worked?

Derek's words sum up the question that most activists are too afraid to ask: are we making a difference?* Is society changing for the better? Pushing Derek's question further: even assuming we have made a difference, is it worth it and at what personal cost?

It's perhaps easier for young people like myself and Derek to throw ourselves deep into activism without another thought – we still live with our parents and don't have much financial burden or

---

* In fact, many of Joshua's fellow Hong Kongers demonstrated against the imposition of the Extradition Bill that led to the summer protests in 2019, when 2 million people – over a quarter of Hong Kong's population – peacefully marched against the law. As a result of the demonstrations, and with the world watching, Carrie Lam was forced to back down, declaring the bill 'dead' on 9 July 2019 and announcing its full withdrawal on 4 September 2019.

family responsibility. What do we have to lose other than our freedom?

By contrast, people like Professor Tai have a different set of considerations. Before Occupy Central he was living a stable, middle-class life, teaching at a leading university and making a comfortable living. Now Professor Tai not only faces a long prison sentence, but also stands to lose his position at the University of Hong Kong and be forced to sell his home to pay for mounting legal bills. Why would any rational person make that kind of sacrifice?

There aren't many people in this world for whom I have unreserved admiration. Professor Benny Tai is one of them.

What Civic Square Means to Me

公民廣場對我的意義

Day 41 – Tuesday, 26 September 2017

As I was getting ready to turn in last night, out of the corner of my eye I spotted a black shape darting away from the foot of my bed. Before I could even react the thing had vanished. To my relief, the giant rat – I assume that's what it was – never appeared again and I was able to have a good night's sleep.

Today is 26 September, exactly 17 days before my 21st birthday. In other words, I only have 16 days left in Pik Uk before my transfer to an adult facility. I wouldn't go so far as to say that time goes by quickly, but having a transfer to break up my six-month sentence (four months assuming good behaviour) does make it feel a bit more tolerable.

I have a number of things to take care of before my transfer. First, I have reams and reams of court documents to rifle through and organise concerning

my appeal. I have no desire to bring all the paperwork with me, since lugging bagfuls of legal
documents into the new facility will draw unneces-
sary attention and raise privacy concerns. I need to
spend a bit of time processing them before passing
everything back to my parents for safekeeping.

Then there are over 200 letters from supporters
that I've read but haven't done anything with. During my parents' visit today my mum said I should
keep the letters and try to reply to them all, however
briefly. She said that's what Nathan has been doing.
It's not bad advice, especially since a few public holidays, including National Day and Mid-Autumn
Festival, are coming up, which will give me plenty
of free time.

Ever since my sentencing, my parents have been
running around for me, working with my lawyers
on the appeal, requesting a deferral at my university
and taking care of all kinds of paperwork and
errands. When a young person goes to prison he
brings the entire family with him. I don't know
where to begin to express my gratitude for everything my parents have done for me.

It looks like I may have to trouble them for one
more thing: there's a possibility that Pik Uk may
hold an open day and invite all parents to visit the
facilities and meet the staff. It turns out that juvenile

prisons regularly organise outreach events to 'bring families together'. Guests will be given a prison tour and asked to sit through long speeches by representatives from the rehabilitation and counselling units.

The open day culminates in a symbolically significant event: a tea ceremony for inmates to prepare and serve tea to their parents. This rather contrived ritual is followed by a 20-minute heart-to-heart between the inmate and his family under the watchful eyes of the guards.

These scenes are frequently depicted in local TV dramas: a child in prison uniform breaks down in front of weeping parents, repents his wayward past, and promises he'll make them proud once he's released. The prison staff will look on with great pride at another reformed soul thanks to their care and guidance.

While that sort of re-education model may work for some inmates, I don't believe it applies to political prisoners who will always believe in their cause. No amount of rehabilitation can make us repent. Even so, I am looking forward to it – if nothing else, it'll be a wonderful opportunity to spend some time with my parents without having a thick window pane between us.

Today is the third anniversary of my Civic Square siege, the event that set in motion the Umbrella Movement and a turning point in my life. This time exactly three years ago, on 26 September 2014, I scaled a metal fence near the government headquarters and called on other protesters to follow me. I was tackled by a dozen police officers and taken into custody. That was my first arrest, which ultimately resulted in my first criminal conviction and prison sentence.

The very name of the place – Civic Square – was coined during my anti-national education campaign in 2012. Before that, the nondescript circular public space was known unimaginatively as the front yard of the Government Headquarters East Wing. It had been sealed off with a metal fence and on the night of my arrest I attempted to reclaim it. So much history has been written in that square since then, and it will always have a special place in my heart.

Operation Black Bauhinia

黑紫荊行動

Day 42 – Wednesday, 27 September 2017

My heart skipped a beat at dinner when I heard the words 'Operation Black Bauhinia' on the news. Don't tell me the Department of Justice is pressing charges for that protest too! I thought.

The Golden Bauhinia was a gift from the Communist Party when Hong Kong was handed back to China in 1997. Every 1 July, also known as Handover Day, the government holds a flag-raising ceremony in the square to commemorate the 'reunification' of Hong Kong with the motherland.

At around 6am on 26 June 2017, roughly seven weeks before my sentencing, myself, Agnes and a number of other activists climbed the 6-metre-high monument and draped a giant black cloth over the Golden Bauhinia. We'd planned the operation ahead of President Xi Jinping's high-profile visit for the

20th anniversary of the Handover to show our opposition to Beijing's increasing intervention in Hong Kong's affairs.

If the DOJ decided to charge us for trespassing or public nuisance, it would be the third criminal case I'd be facing after the unlawful assembly charge for storming Civic Square and the contempt of court for breaching the Mongkok injunction. It would add to my prison term and throw my whole timetable out the window.

It turned out to be a false alarm. The news report had mentioned Black Bauhinia because some of the protesters arrested for the operation had refused bail and were released by police unconditionally. But we're not out of the woods just yet. The DOJ 'reserves the right' to file charges against us in the future, just as they did with Alex, Nathan and me, as well as the Occupy Central Trio, years after the movement ended.

What the DOJ does is entirely beyond our control – the Justice Secretary alone has the power and resources to take criminal actions against us. The authorities are always in the driver's seat, whereas activists can only react to their whims. Whatever the future holds for me, I have to stay focused and remain positive.

Books have helped me do both. I just finished reading *20th Century Chinese History*, published by

Oxford University Press, which dissects contemporary China from both macro (history-based) and micro (event-based) perspectives. It analyses recent political uprisings, including the 1989 Tiananmen Square protests, through the lens of a totalitarian regime, not justifying China's actions but trying to understand its motives and mindset. If I wasn't in jail I wouldn't have the time or patience to labour through a dense academic book like this. Having the opportunity to read is one of the silver linings that give me some solace.

So is getting to know a broad range of people behind bars, like this Vietnamese inmate I met in the main yard today. He's roughly my age and was arrested earlier this year for drug trafficking and illegal entry into Hong Kong. He opened up to me about his upbringing in Vietnam and the events that led him down this path. Until meeting him and other inmates convicted of similar charges, illegal drugs was something I would only hear about through the government's aggressive 'Stand Firm! Knock Drugs Out' campaign. Being here has given context and nuance to what most people consider a black and white issue.

To: Mr Joshua Wong

寄給: 黃之鋒

Day 43 – Thursday, 28 September 2017

I received an unusual letter this morning. It caught my attention because it was addressed to 'Mr Joshua Wong' instead of my prison number. It must have taken a few extra days to get delivered because most prison staff don't even know my Christian name.

The letter came from the United States Senate Committee on Foreign Relations. It was a joint letter from five Democratic and Republican senators expressing solidarity with Alex, Nathan and me and condemning the Hong Kong government for prosecuting non-violent protesters. Both the US Senate seal at the top of the page and the wet ink signatures at the bottom made the piece of paper feel weighty in my hands.

Despite the unprecedented outpouring of support received by the Umbrella Movement around the world, universal suffrage for Hong Kong remains dead in the water. In the years since the uprising Beijing has dug its heels in and taken the topic off the political table. Every time I hear words of encouragement from politicians and scholars overseas, like today's letter, it adds to the conflicting emotions inside me. I feel like we've let everybody down.

But as Alex put it succinctly in a recent letter:

> If the path to democracy was free of obstacles, then Hong Kong would have arrived at the finish line a generation ago and I wouldn't be writing to you from prison. It's precisely because the path is full of obstacles that we've taken up the mantle to continue the unfinished journey.

I know I can always count on good old Alex to get me out of a mental rut.

Joshua and Caleb

約書與亞迦勒

Day 44 – Friday, 29 September 2017

Today went by quickly. I spent the morning in the computer room learning Adobe Illustrator and the afternoon with visitors. By the time I returned to the main yard for group exercises it was almost dinner.

My lawyers had important news today. A date has finally been set for the sentencing hearing for my Mongkok contempt of court case – the second week of October. I took my lawyers' advice to enter a guilty plea for violating a court injunction and now it's up to the judge to decide how and where I will spend the next few months. If luck is on my side I'll either be given a suspended sentence or allowed to serve both my current and the contempt sentences simultaneously. I try not to think too hard about it; I know false hopes can be crushing.

Among the letters I received today was one from Raphael Wong, a friend and one of the NNT Thirteen currently serving time in prison. In it he wrote:

> Remember that night in 2014? You, me, and all those kids from Scholarism and the Federation of Students – we all wanted to find a way to energise the protesters in Admiralty. In the end we decided to storm Civic Square, but you were arrested and I wasn't. And yet here we are. Both ended up behind bars just the same. I think it's destiny.
>
> If you are Joshua, then I must be Caleb. Together we can take the pro-democracy movement forward and lead Hong Kong to the Promised Land!

Raphael and I are both Christians. He knows that my parents named me after Joshua, the prophet who led the Israelites to the promised land of Canaan after Moses' death. My parents weren't thinking about political leadership when they picked the name, but they did want me to be an upstanding citizen who does the right thing and inspires others to do the same. Ever since my parents told me the story of Joshua I've tried my best not to let them down.

According to the Book of Numbers in the Old Testament, Caleb and Joshua worked side by side to explore new land for possible settlement. They famously carried a huge cluster of grapes from Canaan to persuade the Israelites that it was the promised land that they had been searching for over 40 years.

Raphael is being humble by referring to himself as Caleb. He has made significant personal sacrifices for Hong Kong. Other than the nine-month sentence he's currently serving, he faces two other criminal charges: one for inciting others to participate in the Umbrella Movement and the other for breaching a court injunction to stay clear of the Mongkok protest site – the same contempt of court charge as mine.

In the past, pro-democracy political parties have had their differences. Even though we fight for the same cause, interpersonal conflicts and ideological disagreements often get in the way. From time to time Raphael and I argue over strategy and direction. But with so many of us locked up in prison it's time we set aside our differences and work with – and not against – each other.

Prison as Experiential Art

模擬監倉

Day 46 – Sunday, 1 October 2017

I took my mum's advice and spent my day off replying to the hundreds of letters from supporters. I knew I wouldn't be able to finish them all before my transfer, but I had to start somewhere. The other inmates kept themselves busy watching *Kung Fu Hustle*, probably the last good Stephen Chow film before he started churning out 'co-produced' films with mainland Chinese studios.

I hadn't realised that today was National Day until I heard the tired old celebratory speeches and national anthem blasting out from the TV. On the news I saw protesters surrounding the Golden Bauhinia, some holding up placards saying 'Free political prisoners'. I also saw footage of a solidarity march down Hennessy Road and the camera zoomed in on the Demosistō contingent. I saw Demosistian

Tiffany Yuen carrying a banner and shouting 'Step down, Rimsky Yuen!' If it weren't for the Justice Secretary's decision to appeal our original sentences (against the recommendation of his staff, I might add), Alex, Nathan and I would have been out there marching on the streets with the rest of the crowd.

The footage made me want to look for more coverage of Demosistō in the newspapers and I was happy to find two articles in today's *Apple Daily*. The first outlined the latest findings of an ongoing research project we've undertaken in partnership with a group called Liber Research Community, a non-profit organisation that undertakes independent research into Hong Kong's social development. 'Decoding Hong Kong's History' involves dozens of volunteers and university students poring over declassified archival materials here and in the UK documenting the discussions over the future of Hong Kong during the Sino-British handover negotiations in the 1980s.

One of the documents shows that Maria Tam, a barrister-politician who became an ardent Beijing loyalist and a political pariah, had once asked the British government to publish periodic reports to monitor the state of Hong Kong under Chinese rule – an act that in today's Hong Kong would have been considered highly unpatriotic and even subversive.

The fact that our research project continues to uncover shocking revelations and attract media coverage makes me really proud.

The second article was about a street demonstration staged by Demosistians yesterday in an effort to boost the turnout at today's solidarity march. A photograph showed two of our members (I couldn't make out their faces) dressed in prison uniform and squatting inside a papier mâché jail cell. It was a simple yet powerful way to let the public visualise what it's like for young people to be locked up like hardened criminals, and to realise that political imprisonment is no longer an abstract idea that they can brush aside.

Mooncake Season

月餅季節

———

Day 48 – Tuesday, 3 October 2017

Mid-Autumn Festival is a big deal in Hong Kong. It's the cultural equivalent of Thanksgiving in America, a night for families to get together for a big feast followed by a mooncake or two.

To make up for being separated from our loved ones on this special occasion – which is tomorrow, prison prepared treats for us. In addition to grilled fish and a hard-boiled egg for dinner tonight we each received a chicken leg the size of a credit card. Of course it was nothing like the kind of fat, juicy chicken leg you'd get from a street-food stall, but here in prison the surprise treat went a long way to make the day feel more festive.

Then we were told that each of us would be collecting our own mooncake tomorrow night. It was a nice touch, although I find the idea of giving out mooncakes in prison somewhat strange. Every Chinese person grows up with the story that mooncakes were used by the revolutionaries to overthrow Mongolian rule at the end of the Yuan dynasty. On a Mid-Autumn Festival some 700 years ago, rebels put secret messages in baked pastries to evade the authorities and wage a successful uprising against the Mongols. I wonder whether the irony of handing out these subversive treats is lost on prison management.

Earlier today, two new inmates arrived at Pik Uk, which means I'll no longer be the only newcomer doing all the sweeping up in the common areas. It means I'll also get help carrying the heavy milk bottles I have to lug up the stairs from the kitchen to the cells on the fourth floor. Mind you, when I say 'milk', I don't mean the fresh kind people get from the supermarket refrigerator. Here we prepare milk by mixing an inordinate amount of water with a stingy portion of milk powder. It's essentially white-coloured water. Unsurprisingly, the inmates aren't lapping it up.

Sentencing on My 21st Birthday

二十一歲生日的判刑

Day 49 – Wednesday, 4 October 2017

I found out from the news today that the sentencing for my contempt of court case has been set for 13 October, which happens to be my 21st birthday. It's not a bad thing given that it means I'll be able to see a few familiar faces – family, Demosistians, lawyers and other activists.

For logistical reasons, prison management has delayed my transfer to Stanley adult prison by a day. That means on 14 October, the day after I attain legal adulthood, I'll say goodbye to the juvenile inmates here and be bussed out of Pik Uk carrying a small bag of personal belongings and a huge bag of junk food, which I plan to purchase in order to use up my October salary.

I spent much of today going through the 200-page Facebook printout Senia Ng sent to me. I read

Tiffany's heartfelt post describing how she has been coping with Nathan's imprisonment (the two Demosistians have been dating for years), as well as her efforts to push back the Education Bureau's attempt to whitewash sensitive subject matters like the Tiananmen Square Protests from secondary school syllabuses.

There was also a post about Derek's trip to London alongside three pan-democracy lawmakers – Eddie Chu, Ray Chan and Ted Hui – to meet with representatives from Britain's Foreign and Commonwealth Office. It was the first visit of its kind in recent memory and an important step in forging closer relations with foreign governments to draw the world's attention to the situation in Hong Kong.

I was also excited to read about the new line-up of presenters on the popular *Demosistō Student Union* programme, a weekly show on radio D100. In the past, Nathan, Derek and I – being the party's most senior members – would always go on the show. Now that the three of us are either in prison or about to be, it opens up opportunities for more junior members to get some airtime and hone their public speaking skills. In terms of inspiring the next generation of leadership, it's a good thing.

Last Few Days with Inmates

與囚友的最後幾天

Day 50 – Thursday, 5 October 2017

Autumn is upon us. The temperature has dropped by a few degrees and we've all put on our blue T-shirts instead of going topless as we have been the last few weeks. In Hong Kong, everyone prefers chilly weather to the sweltering summer heat.

Yesterday was the Mid-Autumn Festival, which makes today a public holiday (the idea is to give people a day to rest after a night of festivities). At Pik Uk, public holidays operate like Sundays – we get to sit around in the canteen all morning and the classroom all afternoon. To get some fresh air and move around a bit, I decided to go for a jog in the main yard.

We've been getting special treats at mealtimes for three days in a row. We were surprised with Chinese pears, spring rolls and hotdogs at dinner yesterday and this morning we each got a gift pack full of snacks like Cheezels, dried squid and soda crackers. Inside was a note from the Christian Prison Pastoral Association with a short story about Christ's crucifixion, several scriptures from the New Testament and a response slip. Inmates are encouraged to fill out the slip to request a pastoral visit or some religious literature, and to tick the box to 'surrender to Jesus Christ and make Him my Saviour'. I wonder how many inmates read the note and how many simply binned it with the packaging.

For weeks now we've been glued to a TVB crime drama called *Line Walker 2*. TV star Moses Chan plays Mr Black, a fearsome organised crime kingpin. In today's episode (in prison we're one episode behind the live broadcast), Mr Black was shot three times by an assassin at point-blank range. Either he was wearing a bulletproof vest and will survive the gunshots, or TVB is willing to kill off the series' leading man, which is highly unlikely. I suppose we'll find out tomorrow.

Inmates were fired up by the climactic scene when Mr Black threw himself in front of his gang brothers and took three bullets from the assassin. During the ad break everyone talked over each other to brag about their own heroic near-death experiences, trading stories of outrunning the police and using encrypted messages to close deals.

What they left out – and I only found out from one-on-one conversations later on – was that most of them ended up in prison because they were thrown under the bus by their leaders. Those at the bottom of the gang pecking order often end up being the fall guys who 'take one for the team'. No matter how much TV shows and movies in Hong Kong glamorise the Triads, there's no shortage of cowardice and hypocrisy within the gang hierarchy.

I also learned that most inmates decided to join gangs for financial reasons – they needed to put food on the table, especially the ones who were estranged from their parents. It's entirely different from the government's narrative that young people choose to become gang members because they want to look cool or because they've flunked out of school and need to find something to do.

Something else I was surprised to find out is that I'm the only person in the entire juvenile prison who has a Christian name. While most people in Hong Kong go by their English names and like to mix English vocabulary into their everyday conversations, this is not the case in prison. In fact, there are inmates who don't even know the alphabet. This morning when I mentioned that I missed having milk tea at the 'weekend', the response I got was 'Chi-fung, no more English words, okay? Speak Cantonese please!'

Last Letter from Pik Uk

獄中札記

Day 53 – Sunday, 8 October 2017

To my supporters:

In a few days I'll turn 21 and be transferred to an adult prison to serve my remaining sentence.

I've now spent 50 days at Pik Uk. Every day I march, I clean, I go to class, I eat and I go to sleep; it's an endless loop that keeps repeating itself. Prisoners are expected to follow strict orders in an environment designed to erase independent thinking and free will. Every decision here is made for us by an unshakable authority. That's the hardest thing about being in jail.

The Bible teaches us that 'suffering produces perseverance; perseverance, character; and character, hope' (Romans 5:3–4). To make the best of a bad situation I've befriended dozens of inmates at Pik Uk. They've given me a deeper understanding of the social issues facing people my age. I've also tried my best to fight against institutional injustices, from physical abuse to mandatory head shaving. Even though I've been threatened with reprisal for speaking up, I remain undeterred and committed to ensuring fairness and dignity for all.

From the anti-national education campaign to the Umbrella Movement, from Scholarism to Demosistō, from the first demonstration I led in 2012 to my imprisonment in 2017, the past six years have been nothing short of a rollercoaster ride. I believe there's a silver lining to my imprisonment. The last seven weeks have given me a chance to take a step back and reflect on my journey of activism, to take stock of mistakes made and lessons learned, to read more books to better myself, and to thank the people who have walked with me along the way.

Many commentators, especially those from the international press, attribute the Umbrella Movement and the political awakening it engendered to the efforts of a few student activists like myself, Nathan and Alex. But nothing is further from the truth. The true heroes who deserve the credit are the amazing people of Hong Kong who for decades have stood by each other and fought for democracy despite the odds.

But we need their help once again. We need every Hong Kong citizen to direct his or her energy, perseverance and commitment to non-violence towards building a more robust civil society. By the time the next political uprising is upon us (in whatever form it may take), we'll be best positioned to make the most of the opportunity and use it to get us closer to our goal.

Over the last 50 days I've received over 770 letters from supporters around the world. Some of them were from self-proclaimed 'blue ribbons' who opposed the Umbrella Movement. Their words of encouragement, despite their political leanings, are ample proof that if we continue to demonstrate to the public that our motives are pure and unselfish, even those who disagree with us may come around.

From a semi-autonomy to a semi-autocracy, Hong Kong has entered a new era of political oppression. To lose faith now is to let our opponents have the last word. But if we each do our part, together our efforts will amount to a force to be reckoned with. The arc of history will bend towards us if we persist long enough.

Joshua Wong
Pik Uk Prison

Presence of God

主的同在

Day 57 – Thursday, 12 October 2017

Today is my last day as a legal minor.

On the eve of a milestone, I was thrilled to receive a birthday card signed by some 30 pastors and ministry leaders from my church. I was particularly inspired by Reverend Yiu's words:

> *The presence of God transcends prison walls*
> *May His grace free you wherever you are*

I've been going to the same church since I was three. The building itself is one of those heritage structures that seats a thousand and the congregation comprises mainly middle-class families from the neighbourhood. It's your average house of worship in Hong Kong.

With some notable exceptions, like Reverend Chu (one of the Occupy Central Trio), religious leaders tend to stay out of politics. Pastors often steer clear of sensitive topics on the grounds that they need to accommodate congregants of all political stripes. During my anti-national education campaign five years ago, I felt resistance and even disapproval from church seniors, which was disappointing considering the way I've always treated them as my second family.

I should point out that not everyone in my church shares this attitude and some are openly supportive of my activism. I also understand why others are sceptical, since religion and politics never used to mix and they simply don't know what to do with a vociferous youth who makes a career out of questioning authority. Besides, how could a pastor offer any meaningful guidance if he doesn't have a firm grip on the underlying political issues?

The civil awakening brought about by the Umbrella Movement is widespread and irreversible. My worry is that if churches in Hong Kong don't evolve with our shifting political landscape they run the risk of alienating their congregants. This problem will only grow as society becomes more polarised and churchgoers demand that their religious leaders take a stand. At some point, even the most loyal members will vote with their feet and find an alternative where their political views and grievances are listened to.

I heard through the grapevine that my transfer date has been set for Monday, 16 October. As requested, I'll be moved to a non-smoking ward in Stanley Prison. One of the biggest advantages of being at an adult prison is that I'll no longer be required to do those Godforsaken morning marches. In fact, I had my last march this morning and even after all this time I still couldn't get it right. I have trouble remembering even basic drill commands in English, which come out funny through the mouths of our Cantonese-speaking sergeants. Who knew that 'lap-wai-lap' is actually 'left-right-left', that 'tsing step' is 'change step' and 'fee see' is 'freeze'? My English pronunciation isn't perfect but even I can tell that the sergeants are butchering the language. Diction aside, I'll never understand why 'change step' means stomping on the ground with my right foot – the phrase bears absolutely no connection to the action.

But prisons are all about keeping up appearances. Morning marches are shown off to bigwig visitors as the ultimate embodiment of discipline and order. Whenever there's a Justice of the Peace or senior correctional officer on the premises we have to line up like schoolchildren and shout out our responses in unison.

One time a VIP arrived for a prison tour and I spotted a mysterious bird's nest on the hallway outside one of the classrooms. When asked why, the prison guard said, 'We planted the nest there to show our esteemed visitor that Pik Uk inmates are very much in touch with Mother Nature.'

ON 16 OCTOBER 2017, JOSHUA WAS TRANSFERRED TO STANLEY PRISON, A MAXIMUM SECURITY ADULT FACILITY.

Blue vs Yellow

藍絲黃絲

Day 66 – Saturday, 21 October 2017

Saturday is a work day at an adult prison. For me, that means more toilets to clean.

I've decided to skip both breakfast and lunch every day until my release. I want to save my appetite for the real food outside. Real food with friends and family.

A few cellmates told me today that the mood has changed around here since my arrival. They said that the staff are more on guard and on edge. Rules that are usually not enforced are suddenly taken much more seriously.

For instance, because of the diversity of inmates, Caucasians are given Western-style meals, South Asians get naan bread and curry, and so on. Non-ethnic Chinese often trade food for purposes of variety and as a social bonding activity. Even though prison guidelines prohibit food sharing (perhaps to prevent inmates from using it as a currency to barter for other things), the guards usually look the other way. After all, what's the harm of a few guys sharing a bite together? But all that has stopped since I got here and the guards are patrolling the canteen nearly every day to make sure it doesn't happen.

Inmate diversity goes beyond ethnicity; there's a huge variety of political views too. The younger prisoners tend to be 'yellow ribbons' supportive of the pro-democracy movement. Several of them have opened up to me about their involvement in the Umbrella Movement and subsequent protests. But there are plenty of hardcore 'blue ribbons' too. Yesterday someone from the Security Unit pulled me aside and told me that some older guys in the workshop had heckled me and yelled 'traitor' when I walked past. I didn't hear them, but I'm hardly surprised.

I received letters from a few university classmates today. We started in the same year and now they're about to graduate. By summer next year they'll be starting their first jobs and getting their first pay slips. Some of them will become architects, others will go into finance or IT. They'll be climbing the corporate ladder and moving ahead in life.

By contrast, I've just deferred my studies for another six months, which puts my earliest possible graduation date at May 2020. And then what? Politics is all I want to do and to be honest all I can do. No company or government department will ever dare come near this thorn in Beijing's side. That's the cold reality of being an activist in Hong Kong.

Path to Full Democracy

香港的民主路

Day 67 – Sunday, 22 October 2017

Since September Catalonia's independence referendum has been in the news nearly every day. The movement reached a fever pitch this week and the 24-hour news channel showed the same footage of massive street protests in Barcelona throughout the day. The more I learn about the Catalan people's demands, the more I feel we have in common.

I'm not talking about Hong Kong independence – I've never advocated for that in the past and I'm not going to now. What I'm referring to is the similarity between Catalonia's efforts to assert its cultural and political identity and Hong Kong's own struggle to do the same in the shadow of Communist China. Many issues we face in Hong Kong, from ever-increasing intervention by the central government to the marginalisation of our mother tongue and the persecution of political activists, will sound as familiar to a Catalan as a Hong Konger.

There's no shortage of popular support within Catalonia for its resistance against Madrid. Turnouts at street protests are always substantial, despite the threat of violence and arrest. What the movement lacks, however, is support from the international community. In the absence of key allies such as overseas governments and the European Union, it's hard to imagine that the Catalan movement will prevail in the near future.

The same lesson applies to our pro-democracy struggle. Pitted against the world's most powerful autocracy, Hong Kong must look globally and secure international support regardless of our demands, be it universal suffrage or some form of self-determination. That's why I've made international interaction and networking a top priority for Demosistō. I hope other pan-democracy political parties will see it too and work with us to find allies overseas.

On a lighter note, a cellmate recorded last Sunday's movie on TVB Pearl and the entire cell cheered when we learned that it was *Avengers: Age of Ultron*. Even though I'd already watched it in the theatre, being a superhero fanboy who's watched every single Marvel and DC movie (some more than once) I was as thrilled as everyone else. Seeing the Marvel logo at the start of the film alone was enough to give me goosebumps. I've already made a mental note to watch the latest *Thor* movie as soon as I'm out of here.

Last Day

最後一天

Day 68 – Monday, 23 October 2017

My last day in prison came and went like any other. I spent the day reading the news, scrubbing toilets and watching a bit of TV with my cellmates. It's fitting that I finished Malala's memoir just before my release. Holding the paperback in my hands, I couldn't help but feel both fortunate and humbled to be able to follow my beliefs and live out my dreams – however far-fetched they first appeared – and make a mark in history.

By the time I'm released I'll have spent 69 days behind bars. While these 69 days are a mere footnote in our decades-long struggle for democracy, they represent an important milestone in my seven-year journey in political activism. Prison has taken away my freedom, but it has given me many things too: time to reflect, space to grow and memories that will last a lifetime. What's more, I'll come out of prison stronger and more committed to our cause than ever.

In many countries around the world, the fight for freedom and democracy puts safety and even lives at risk. As my Pakistani cellmate rightly pointed out, the cost of activism in other places is much higher than what we face in Hong Kong.* Yet that can change quickly, as we've witnessed with the conviction of the '13 plus 3'. It's all the more reason for us to make as much progress and generate as much momentum while we still can, before the cost of resistance becomes prohibitively high. We have no excuse not to and we owe it to future generations to at least try.

This will be my last journal entry, at least for now. I'll be back within these walls soon enough. Our struggle is far from over.

---

* The situation in Hong Kong has deteriorated rapidly since Joshua's imprisonment in 2017. *See Act III, Chapter 1, The Extradition Bill Crisis.*

ACT III

THE THREAT TO GLOBAL DEMOCRACY

'Injustice anywhere is a threat to justice everywhere.'
—Martin Luther King Jr

The Extradition Bill Crisis: A Global Trend in Citizen-based Democracy

逃犯條例危機: 公民民主的全球趨勢

A lot has happened in Hong Kong since my first incarceration.

If I were to liken our epic struggle for freedom and democracy to the original *Star Wars* trilogy, then the two years since my imprisonment in 2017 would be a drawn-out version of the middle instalment: *The Empire Strikes Back*. While the Resistance was still regrouping and recovering from the last political uprising, the Imperial Fleet led by the new chief executive Carrie Lam had begun an all-out counter-attack on civil society.

In January 2018, three months after I walked out of Stanley Prison, the election authorities barred Demosistian spokeswoman Agnes Chow from running in the by-election to fill Nathan's vacated LegCo seat. The ban was issued on the grounds that Demosistō's self-determination stance was seditious and not in line with the Basic Law.

The announcement came after Agnes had already renounced her British citizenship in order to run for office, which meant the sacrifice she had made against her parents' wishes was for nothing. When I offered her my apologies she said, without a hint of regret, 'I'm a big girl. I knew what I was getting myself into; besides, don't make a habit of apologising for things the government has done to us.'

And the bad news kept coming. In April, after months of gruelling court trials, nine prominent activists involved in the Umbrella Movement were convicted on public nuisance and incitement charges. While some of them received suspended or community-service sentences, Professors Benny Tai and Chan Kin-man of the Occupy Central Trio were each sentenced to 16 months in prison, while 'Bottle' Shiu Ka-chun and Raphael Wong each received 8-month sentences.

Then, in July, the Department of Security took the unprecedented move to ban a political party, the Hong Kong National Party, for its pro-independence stance. Less than a week later, the government deported Victor Mallet of the *Financial Times* for hosting the founder of the banned party for a talk at the Foreign Correspondents' Club. It was the first expulsion of a foreign correspondent on political grounds in the city's history.

By shutting the opposition out of the legislature and locking its people up when they took to the streets, the Hong Kong government was forcing its opponents to pursue more radical options. No one else but our political leaders, who act at the behest of the Chinese Communist Party, is responsible for pushing citizens towards more violent forms of resistance, destabilising the city in the process. As activists, our challenge is to strike the delicate balance between principles and results, means and ends. What else can we do when our right to political participation is denied to us and non-violent protests are repeatedly ignored? How much violence, if any, can be tolerated to further our cause without alienating Hong Kong society and the international community?

We didn't have to wait long before we had to confront these questions head on. In June 2019, on the heels of the 30th anniversary of the Tiananmen Square Massacre and nearly five years after the Umbrella Movement brought Hong Kongers out onto the streets, the city was once again mired in political unrest. A controversial fugitive transfer arrangement with China tabled by the government set off a fresh round of large-scale protests. What followed was something that nobody – not the pro-democracy camp, not Carrie Lam's administration, and certainly not the Communist leadership in Beijing – could have imagined.

At the heart of the firestorm was a government proposal that would allow the extradition of criminal suspects to stand trial on the mainland. Many feared that anyone in Hong Kong, from the local business-man to the foreigner working in, or simply passing through, the city, could be arrested and delivered to the authorities across the border where a fair trial and due process are not guaranteed. The disparity between their judicial systems and legal safeguards is the reason why most modern democracies, such as the United States, the United Kingdom, Germany and Japan, have refused to enter into extradition treaties with China. In fact, this very issue was brought up during the Handover negotiations; a mutual fugitive transfer arrangement between Hong Kong and China was specifically excluded from our extradition ordinances because of concerns over potential political persecution and human rights abuses.

As soon as the Extradition Bill was announced, civil society was up in arms over the proposal's potentially chilling effect on free expression in Hong Kong; China is known to punish critics by fabricating criminal charges such as tax evasion and drug trafficking against them. The bill came within weeks of the high-profile arrest by Canadian authorities of Meng Wanzhou, CFO of Chinese tech giant Huawei. The timing had the city's expat community worried about retaliatory actions by Beijing via the extradition channel. 'If this dangerous bill gets passed,' a Chinese-American friend said to me, 'the Communists can get their hands on anyone they don't like. They can do it openly and legally without resorting to kidnapping like they did to the booksellers!'

Distrust of Beijing aside, what Hong Kongers found even more infuriating was Carrie Lam's stubborn determination to press ahead with the bill in the face of public outcry. Her intransigence had everyone asking: why is she so fixated on an arrangement that nobody wants, when society is already divided as it is and there are other, much more pressing, issues like housing and old-age poverty? Is this Beijing's idea or her own pet project designed to impress her bosses? Regardless of the answers, the self-inflicted crisis confirmed Lam's image as a tone-deaf career bureaucrat and underscored the problems of an unelected government.

When mass protests began to flare up in June, it felt as if it was the Umbrella Movement all over again, except this time protesters were angrier and more combative than their predecessors. Young people's voices went from loud to deafening as they refused to be brushed aside in the way they had been in 2014. Street demonstrations escalated quickly after two back-to-back million-person marches failed to move the political needle – both the Hong Kong and Chinese governments refused to scrap the Extradition Bill despite the record-breaking turnouts. Peaceful rallies soon gave way to full-scale urban guerrilla warfare.

A more militant breed of protester emerged, dressed in black and wearing yellow hard hats and half-face respirator masks, and the movement grew in size and organisation. Faceless and leaderless, it self-mobilised using crowdsourcing apps and began clashing with police and vandalising properties of businesses perceived to be pro-establishment. Some dug up bricks from the pavement and hurled them at the police, while others threw Molotov cocktails and set subway exits on fire. A piece of anti-government graffiti offered a poignant explanation, if not a justification, for the use of more aggressive tactics: 'It was YOU who taught us that peaceful protest doesn't work!'

In response, the police unleashed an unprecedented use of force on protesters, hitting them with rubber bullets, stun grenades, bean-bag rounds, water cannons and even live ammunition. To make matters worse, hired thugs jumped into the fray to beat up demonstrators and passers-by alike, while police officers stood idly by or escorted the assailants away. All this pushed anti-police sentiment to an all-time high. If Carrie Lam resembled Darth Vader, then the Hong Kong Police Force would be the armour-clad, blaster-brandishing stormtroopers terrorising villagers across the galaxy.

I will never forget the night in July when protesters confronted a phalanx of riot police in Sheung Wan, a stone's throw from the city's financial heart. Shortly after midnight, law enforcement began an operation to clear the area by firing a rapid succession of tear-gas rounds into the crowds, turning the quiet residential enclave into a smoke-filled battlefield. Nathan and I were on the frontline hoping to reason with the officer in command, but to no avail. We had trouble breathing and started coughing uncontrollably, our paper-thin surgical masks useless against the engulfing smoke. We tried to outrun the volleys of tear gas but there was just too much of it all around us. 'This is it – I'm going to suffocate and die,' I thought to myself, before Nathan found a way out and pulled me to safety.

In September, three months after non-stop violent clashes turned Hong Kong into an urban war zone, Carrie Lam finally relented and announced the full withdrawal of the Extradition Bill. But her concession was dismissed by protesters as 'too little, too late' and did nothing to quell public anger. By then, the anti-extradition campaign had already evolved into a broader movement for accountability and democracy; the battle cry on the streets had changed from 'No extradition to China' and 'Kill the bill' to 'Liberate Hong Kong; revolution of our times!' and 'Five demands, not one less.' Among the five demands were the creation of an independent commission to investigate police misconduct, amnesty for arrested protesters and universal suffrage.

In many ways this new round of popular uprising is part of a larger global trend of citizen-driven democracy. From the Czech Republic and Russia to Iran, Kazakhstan and Ethiopia, ordinary citizens are using what little freedom of expression they have at their disposal to voice their frustrations over corruption, failed economic policies and regression in civil liberties. Halfway around the world in Venezuela, for instance, President Nicolás Maduro's move towards a one-man rule by filling both the legislature and the courts with political allies and the subsequent collapse of the Venezuelan economy brought massive crowds to the streets demanding his resignation. Most recently in Chile, violent demonstrations against a subway fare increase morphed into a full-blown popular uprising demanding social equality. Similarly, in Lebanon protesters occupied major thoroughfares in the capital city of Beirut to oppose a series of proposed taxes and other austerity measures.

Meanwhile, some resistance movements are so powerful, and their concerns so universal, that they transcend geographical boundaries and galvanise citizens the world over. Extinction Rebellion, or XR, for instance, began in the UK in May 2018 to demand immediate government action to address climate change and treat it like the existential crisis it is. In the 18 months since its start the movement has spread to over 60 cities on 5 continents and inspired legions of 'XR Youth' to join the fight, thanks in large part to powerful voices like the Swedish teenage activist Greta Thunberg. Many of these grassroots movements, from XR to the post-Parkland gun-law campaign in the United States, are increasingly led by millennials and Generation Zers, as they are often the ones most impacted by older generations' inaction and acquiescence.

Whether it is the developed or the developing world, bottom-up resistance made possible by social networks and crowdsourcing tools is slowly but steadily coalescing into a formidable 'fifth estate' holding the ruling class to account. When the three branches of government – executive, legislative and judicial – are no longer effective in safeguarding democratic values, and the fourth estate of the free press is being targeted and silenced with growing intensity, a fifth power emerges to provide the necessary checks and balances on those in power.

Hong Kong is a case in point. The executive branch, including the head of government, is handpicked by Beijing to do its bidding. The legislature, already stacked with pro-establishment loyalists, has been rendered even more powerless with the wanton disqualification of opposition lawmakers. The independent judiciary, once the pride of Hong Kong and a bedrock for its economic prosperity, is being undermined by frequent overrulings by the National People's Congress, China's central legislative body. In the meantime, pro-Beijing businesses are exerting pressure on media outlets by pulling advertising or gobbling them up altogether, as was the case in the acquisition of the *South China Morning Post* by Chinese e-commerce giant Alibaba with the explicit goal to present China in a positive light. Where the other four powers have failed, a citizen-driven fifth estate comes in to fill the void. This global pattern of a mass protest movement acting as a counterweight to the state is best captured in a line from the dystopian film *V for Vendetta*: 'People should not be afraid of their governments. Governments should be afraid of their people.'

As Hong Kong plunged deeper and deeper into chaos, I became more convinced than ever that we could not fight this battle alone. Our embattled city needed a global influencer to rally overseas support and lobby foreign governments to put pressure on both our own government and Beijing. I was ready to step into that role. In September I travelled to Washington DC to testify in front of the US Congressional-Executive Commission on China (CECC). I was accompanied by Denise Ho, Canto-pop star turned human rights activist, and Demosistian Jeffrey Ngo.

Jeffrey is a Washington-based PhD student at Georgetown University and Demosistō's de facto foreign liaison. Jeffrey has written nearly all of my speeches on my foreign trips – his English is much stronger than mine – and the two of us have collaborated on numerous op-eds in international publications such as the *Guardian*, the *Wall Street Journal* and *Time*.

The focus of the CECC hearing, titled 'Hong Kong's Summer of Discontent and US Policy Responses', was twofold: first, to address the spiralling social unrest sparked by the Extradition Bill; and second, to rally support for the passing of the

Hong Kong Human Rights and Democracy Act of 2019. Once passed, the act will enable the US government to, among other things, sanction high-ranking government officers like Carrie Lam and Secretary for Security John Lee, as well as members of the Hong Kong Police Force responsible for violent crackdowns on protesters. The US government may deny entry to sanctioned individuals and freeze their onshore assets. A second bill called the PRO-TECT Hong Kong Act was also introduced. This bill aims to stop American exports of crowd control weapons to Hong Kong.

During the hearing I worked hard to explain the gravity of the situation in Hong Kong. 'The recent political crisis has turned a global city into a police state,' I said. 'I would describe the situation as a collapse of "one country, two systems". Now is the time to seek bipartisan support for the democratisation of Hong Kong. It isn't a matter of left or right, but a matter of right or wrong.'

It was heartening to be granted an audience by political heavyweights like Senator Marco Rubio and CECC Chairman and House Representative Jim McGovern. It was equally encouraging to speak in a room full of overseas Hong Kongers. The massive turnout was in stark contrast with a similar congressional hearing I attended five years ago during the Umbrella Movement, where Jeffrey was pretty much the only person from Hong Kong in the audience. We've come a long way in generating support and attention from Hong Kongers living abroad.

I ended my testimony with a solemn plea: 'Now is the time for the US Congress to pass the Hong Kong Human Rights and Democracy Act. I also hope that the US government will prioritise human rights issues when it reviews its policy on China.'

After the hearing, Denise, Jeffrey and I were ushered to another chamber, where House Speaker Nancy Pelosi and Foreign Affairs Committee Chairman Eliot Engel awaited us for a press conference under a giant portrait of George Washington. After we addressed the press, Speaker Pelosi gave me a hug and said, 'You are an inspiration to young people everywhere. Thank you for your courage and resolve.' This was the same fearless congresswoman who protested on Tiananmen Square in 1991 with a banner bearing the words 'To those who die for democracy in China', and who went on to become the most powerful woman in American politics. I am grateful that we have her and other powerful figures in the international community rooting for Hong Kong and fighting our corner.

As the three of us left Capitol Building we were heckled by a throng of angry mainland Chinese demonstrators who were being held back behind a police line. They yelled 'Traitors!' and 'Running dogs!' while waving Chinese flags and punching in the air. I looked the loudest ones in the eye and said, in Mandarin, 'Take a deep breath of this air of freedom in America. You don't get much of it back home.'

Square Peg in a Round Hole: The Countdown to 2047

方枘圓鑿: 倒數 2047

In the early summer of 2016, for a single minute every night the facade of the tallest building in Hong Kong, the International Commerce Centre (ICC), transformed into a giant digital timer. Second by second, the clock counted down to 1 July 2047, the expiration date of the 'one country, two systems' framework that guarantees Hong Kong's semi-autonomy. The light installation was the handiwork of two young local artists who wanted to express their anxiety over the looming deadline and Beijing's tightening grip on the city. Once the building's management realised the subversive message, the ICC cancelled the light show and distanced itself from the artwork. But the artists had already achieved their goal: images of the so-called 'countdown machine' had been plastered across social media and in newspapers the world over.

There is the colonial-era cliché that Hong Kong is a borrowed place on borrowed time. Like all clichés, this one contains a measure of truth. Before the Handover, nervous citizens counted down to the end of British rule. As soon as the clock struck midnight on 30 June 1997, a 50-year timer began to tick. To its 7.5 million inhabitants, Hong Kong is one big rental unit and we are its tenants. Nothing ever belongs to us completely or permanently.

But we don't need to wait until 2047 to know that something isn't quite right. Two decades into the sovereignty transfer, the real impact of Chinese rule, however innocuous it first appeared, has finally registered. Citizens are coming to the realisation that 'one country, two systems' is more a myth than a promise. Popular uprisings in recent years, from the Umbrella Movement to the still-unfolding Extradition Bill crisis, have underscored the inherent contradictions within the framework: how can anyone trust a totalitarian state to run or even tolerate a free society?

'Hong Kongers have been taken in by the Chinese Communist Party,' I often say to foreigners who ask me what I think of 'one country, two systems'. 'The CCP doesn't understand liberal values, let alone embrace them. It's as paradoxical as the United States running a communist territory on its soil.'

Any way you cut it, a democratic Hong Kong under Chinese rule is as out of place as a square peg in a round hole.

China and Hong Kong haven't always been at odds with each other. It's hard to imagine that there was actually a time, not too long ago, when mother and child were on good terms. After the British colony transitioned into a special administrative region without a hitch, citizens began to see their destiny intertwined with that of their mainland brothers and sisters. They believed that if China prospered, so would Hong Kong, and vice versa. Cross-border economic integration wasn't only an inevitability, it was also an opportunity. Many who had fled Hong Kong before 1997 decided to return; some even moved to the mainland in search of better wages and advancement prospects.

After the SARS outbreak in 2003, the central government relaxed travel restrictions for mainlanders to visit Hong Kong in an effort to revive our slumped economy with tourism dollars. Grateful citizens who had been traumatised by a deadly disease welcomed them with open arms. After a catastrophic 8.0-magnitude earthquake levelled parts of Sichuan Province in 2008, Hong Kongers returned the favour and paid it forward. They opened their hearts and wallets, donating hundreds of millions in aid and provisions. The first Sunday after the disaster, my church congregation observed a moment of silence to honour earthquake victims and set up donation boxes all around the premises.

A semblance of patriotism among citizens started to emerge. It continued to grow and peaked during the 2008 Beijing Olympics, China's coming-out party to the world. Hong Kongers flocked to the capital to root for their 'home team', waving the Five-starred Red Flag and chanting 'Add oil, China!' meaning 'Go for it!' I was 11 years old at the time and one of my classmates who had gone to the games gave me a keychain with a Fuwa, the official mascot. He showed me pictures of him posing in front of the iconic Water Cube aquatics centre; the entire family was wearing matching 'I Heart China' T-shirts.

But the flash of China pride didn't last. The massive, unrestrained influx of cross-border visitors started to snarl traffic and the city gradually devolved into a giant duty-free shop for mainlanders. Retail rents skyrocketed and beloved local restaurants and family shops gave way to faceless skincare chains and pharmacies to attract the red dollar. Worse, Hong Kong became a haven for well-heeled Chinese businessmen and high-ranking officials to hide their fortunes from the authorities, bidding up property prices in the process. In the ten-year period before the Umbrella Movement, residential property prices more than doubled and Hong Kong was the world's most expensive city in which to buy a home year after year.

Our everyday grievances told only half the story. Since President Xi Jinping took power in 2012, Beijing's grip on Hong Kong society has gone from tight to choking. From the 31 August framework that dashed our hopes for universal suffrage to the booksellers' abductions, Oathgate and political imprisonment, Hong Kongers can feel the political ground simultaneously shifting and shrinking beneath their feet. Successive political showdowns bear out the notion that Hong Kong has not and will never shed its colony status. We've simply been handed from one imperialist master to another.

The growing sense of unbelonging towards the motherland contributed to a collective identity crisis. Survey after survey has shown that citizens, especially the youth, are distancing themselves from the 'Chinese' label and increasingly identifying themselves as 'Hong Kongers', 'Hong Kong people', or any other appellation that doesn't contain the 'C word'. This 'anything but Chinese' sentiment swelled as a new identity was being forged. This new self-image is best captured in the protest anthem from the recent Extradition Bill crisis, titled 'Glory to Hong Kong':

> *When the dawn comes*
>   *we shall liberate Hong Kong*
> *Brother and sisters walk arm in arm*
>   *in the revolution of our times*
> *Our quest for freedom and democracy will not falter*
> *May glory be to Hong Kong*

The love-and-hate relationship between mother and child is a two-way street. As much as Hong Kongers view Communist China with distrust and disdain, Communist China, too, is re-evaluating its approach to running Hong Kong. China's accession to the World Trade Organization – and the breakneck economic growth that followed – means Hong Kong is not nearly as financially and strategically important to Beijing as it once was. In fact, China has made a concerted effort since the Handover to groom Shanghai and Shenzhen as viable replacements to the wayward child. More and more multinationals are bypassing Hong Kong and setting up regional headquarters on the mainland, despite the many perils of doing business in China, from intellectual property theft to the lack of rule of law.

To the Communist leadership, Hong Kong is no longer the proverbial goose that lays the golden egg. What was once a gateway to China is now perceived by Beijing as a burgeoning base of subversion. Both the Umbrella Movement and the Extradition Bill crisis are viewed as open challenges to Chinese rule. If left unchecked, freewheeling dissent may spread to the mainland and threaten the very stability of the Communist regime. By Beijing's calculations, the special administrative region is more trouble than it's worth, and the only way to rein in what the leadership regards as a bunch of Westernised cry-babies is to keep them in a state of perpetual adolescence, never allowing them to achieve political maturity.

This mutual distrust and disdain are the backdrop against which Hong Kong heads toward 2047. The prognosis for the remaining 20 or so years is grim, as repression begets defiance and defiance begets more repression. This gloomy outlook is not lost on us. Already a second exodus is underway as Hong Kongers flee the city en masse like their parents did in the 1980s and 90s. In the past two years since I was in prison, many relatives and family friends have uprooted their lives and moved overseas. These days, local bookstores are filled with titles like *Hong Kongers' Guide to Opening a Café in*

Taiwan and *Emigration to Europe for Dummies.* The same conversations my parents' generation used to have in their twenties and thirties are once again heard around the dinner table and at the office drinks machine: 'How does the Australian point system work? Will my score go up if I purchase a property?' or 'You should leave now while your kids are still small, they'll assimilate better and learn to speak English without an accent.'

Nearly halfway through its 50-year countdown, Hong Kong is at an existential crossroads. The assumption that half a century is plenty of time for Communist China to democratise or at least meet us halfway in terms of political reform has been spectacularly disproved. Come 2047, the city will either stay put – if Beijing thinks it serves its interests to renew the 'one country, two systems' policy – or, more likely, fully integrate with the rest of China in a 'one country, one system' scenario. Based on the current trajectory, the popular lament that 'Hong Kong will become just another mainland city' seems inescapable. The other two options – that Hong Kongers will achieve total independence or outlive the Communist regime as Eastern Europe did with the Soviet Union – both appear implausible given China's seemingly unstoppable rise to economic and political dominance.

But no matter how grim the future looks, I refuse to give in to the growing sense that there is nothing we can do and that Hong Kong is finished. As the clock ticks down to 2047, I am more convinced than ever that our quest for freedom and democracy will prevail in the end. My optimism is rooted not only in my conviction that democracy is an inevitable global movement, one that even the most formidable regime cannot reverse, but also in my unshakable faith in the people of Hong Kong. We are united by our courage, tenacity, resilience, ingenuity, resourcefulness and sense of purpose, summed up in a single phrase long used to describe the core essence of Hong Kongers: the 'Lion Rock spirit'. It is the collective belief that we can overcome any adversity if we try hard enough, a belief inspired by the namesake mountain that has been watching over our land since time immemorial.

So don't count us out just yet. Throughout our history, every sceptic that's prophesied the end of Hong Kong – during the Japanese occupation in World War II, at the reassumption of power by China at the turn of the millennium, when a deadly epidemic swept through the city in 2003 and a full-scale popular uprising rocked its foundations in 2014 – has been proven wrong. No matter the obstacles, the city will achieve political maturity and reach its full potential as a beacon of resilience and defiance around the world. I am sure of it.

I will be exactly 50 years old in 2047. I want to be able to tell my children that their father once fought a good fight to safeguard their homeland. I will tell them that their father didn't make the same mistake their grandparents' generation did at the Handover, when they let other parties decide their own future.

One World, Two Empires: A New Cold War

兩雄相爭: 新冷戰思為

On 1 October 2019, the Chinese Communist Party commemorated the 70th anniversary of the founding of the People's Republic of China. The day-long celebration culminated in a massive military parade on Tiananmen Square, the largest of its kind in the party's history. As fighter jets zoomed overhead in perfect fly-past formations, a convoy of nuclear-capable missiles and other never before seen weapon systems rumbled down Chang'an Avenue under the watchful eye of President Xi Jinping. During his speech, Xi declared to thunderous applause, 'The Chinese people have risen! No force can stop China and its people from forging ahead!'

For decades, since Deng Xiaoping's 'reform and openness' initiative began in 1978 – the economic version of Gorbachev's Glasnost and Perestroika that sought to reform the Soviet Union in the early 1980s – and the Tiananmen Square Massacre that nearly derailed it, the free world has operated on the assumption that economic prosperity will bring about political reform in Communist China. As quality of life improves, it is argued, the Chinese people will become more educated and connected with the rest of the world. They will demand more freedoms and accountability from those in power, forcing the latter to modernise and democratise the country's political system. The formula has worked elsewhere in Asia, for example in South Korea and Taiwan, and so why not China? Time and money, too, will run their course in the 'Middle Kingdom'.

Deng's successors, Jiang Zemin and Hu Jintao, stuck to the formula to a large extent. They were aggressive on economic growth and relatively moderate on nationalist fervour and ideological control. It was on this basis that China was admitted to the World Trade Organization in 2003 and cemented its status as 'The Factory of the World'. The 2008 Beijing Olympics was China's way of telling the world that it was every bit the benevolent economic powerhouse that it claimed to be, and that its 'peaceful rise' was not only good for its people, it was also good for the world.

Then, in 2012, everything changed when Xi Jinping beat out his political rivals in the once-a-decade leadership change and ascended to the role of Paramount Leader. The son of a prominent revolutionary who had fought side-by-side with Mao during the Chinese Civil War, Xi is a wolf in panda's clothing, whose gentle, understated public persona belies ambition and ruthlessness. Since assuming the throne he has sought to secure a place next to Mao in the pantheon of powerful Communist leaders. In 2017, Xi manoeuvred to have his political theory enshrined into the Chinese constitution alongside the teachings of Mao and Deng. A few months later, he engineered a constitutional amendment to remove presidential term limits, effectively crowning himself Emperor for Life.

Domestically, Xi has successfully consolidated power by purging political rivals using a nationwide anti-corruption campaign and crushing dissent on the pretext of social harmony. The Chinese government has deployed face recognition, online surveillance and other cutting-edge technology to monitor its citizens and manipulate public opinion. Hundreds of human rights lawyers have been arrested and charged with inciting subversion. Catholic congregations are routinely harassed and pushed underground as their churches are raided and demolished, while Tibetans have been stripped of their freedom of speech, religion and movement. In Xinjiang Province, as many as 3 million Uighur

Muslims have been imprisoned or sent to re-education camps.

Internationally, China has been flexing its military muscle by building artificial islands as naval and air bases in the South China Sea, unnerving neighbours like Malaysia, Indonesia and the Philippines. The country has grown markedly more assertive in territorial disputes with Japan, India and Vietnam. The Chinese government has also been accused of launching coordinated cyberattacks on government networks and research agencies in the US, Canada, Australia and India.

This show of hard power is matched by a full-scale sharp-power offensive. China has been wielding its growing financial and cultural influence to entice, coerce, manipulate and bully other countries into acquiescence and cooperation. It has set up hundreds of Confucius Institutes around the world to spread propaganda under the guise of language teaching and cultural exchange. Under the auspices of its ambitious Belt and Road Initiative (BRI), China has been aggressively pitching its infrastructure-based economic model to countries from Myanmar and Sri Lanka to Kazakhstan and Cyprus. Multi-billion dollar construction contracts awarded to Chinese companies are often fraught with corruption and financed with crushing debt that serves to increase China's political leverage over the foreign government.

The combination of carrot and stick in regional diplomacy has allowed China to export far more than manufactured goods and infrastructure know-how. Increasingly, Xi is seeking to spread his own brand of one-party rule in Asia and beyond, just as the Soviet Union sought to spread communism in the Cold War era. Chinese companies have been marketing and selling citizen surveillance systems, euphemistically known as 'smart city' technology, to autocracies in the Middle East and Latin America. Beijing's economic assistance to and open endorsement of North Korea and Myanmar are a key reason why these brutal regimes continue to operate with impunity despite international condemnation and isolation.

China's unprecedented economic clout and political stature have made many governments, especially its neighbours in Asia, its allies and enablers. One example hit particularly close to home. In October 2016, while I was on my way to give a talk on youth activism at Chulalongkorn University in Bangkok, I was detained by Thai authorities at the airport without being given any reason. During my confinement in a dark cell, one of the officials told me in broken English, 'This is Thailand, not Hong

Kong. Thailand is just like China!' He was referring to the lack of human rights protection in both countries. Those were by far the scariest hours in my life, not only because of the language barrier, but also because I was on foreign soil without access to a lawyer. Worse, the incident happened on the heels of the Causeway Bay bookseller abductions. One of the abductees had vanished while on holiday in Pattaya, a beach resort in Thailand. Even though I was released after 12 hours and sent back to Hong Kong on the same day, the episode was a wake-up call to me that Beijing's long arm has reached far beyond its soil and that many foreign governments have been cowed into doing its bidding. Today, my mobility in the region continues to be highly restricted; I can count all the places in Asia I consider it safe for me to travel to on one hand: Japan, South Korea and Taiwan.

By now, any pretence that China is on a peaceful rise to superpower status has been shattered once and for all. The world's second most powerful nation is contributing to a troubling global trend where autocratic regimes are encroaching on democratic rights both domestically and internationally. We have seen Russia, another authoritarian superpower, clamp down on anti-government activists at home and annex Crimea from neighbouring Ukraine.

Similarly, Narendra Modi's government in India has attempted to silence the opposition at home and invaded semi-autonomous Kashmir, just as the Turkish military regime has imprisoned journalists and displaced millions of Kurds in northern Syria.

Their motivation is singular: self-perpetuation. To consolidate and maintain power domestically these regimes have shown no compunction about crushing dissenters, crippling civil society and removing other obstacles that stand in their way. Outside their borders they flex their military muscles to make a show of strength abroad and, more crucially, to impress and intimidate their home audiences. These twin offensives are critical because autocratic regimes are often embroiled in factional infighting centrally while battling popular insurgencies regionally. However invincible and invulnerable they appear to the outside world, the two-front strategy is the only way for them to retain power and prolong its existence. China's simultaneous territorial expansion abroad and brutal crackdown on minorities and human rights activists at home are a case in point.

But that's not all. President Xi's continent-spanning Belt and Road Initiative suggests an even greater ambition: to challenge America's dominance in world trade and global diplomacy. In many ways, the 'one country, two systems' formula for Hong Kong is also how the Communist leadership views its relationship with the rest of the world. In his grand vision of a new global order, Xi is advancing a 'one world, two empires' framework in which the United States and its allies defend their liberal, rights-based ideology, while China and other one-party states demand non-interference from the free world and quietly pursue an oppressive and expansionary agenda. BRI is a thinly veiled attempt to create a strategic blockade to counter the US-led alliance system with Japan, South Korea, the Philippines, Taiwan and Australia that has been the bulwark of East Asian security since World War II.

A new cold war is brewing between China and the rest of the democratic world, and Hong Kong is holding the line in one of its first battles. Nothing captures that tension more vividly than the surreal 'split-screen' moments on 1 October 2019 when live coverage of the 70th anniversary celebrations in Beijing was shown side by side with scenes of anti-government demonstrators braving tear gas and throwing eggs at Xi's portraits on the streets of Hong Kong. The contrast between the two narratives not only symbolises the David-versus-Goliath struggle of Hong Kongers against a regime that is infinitely more powerful, it also sends a clear message to the world that China's tightening grip on Hong Kong is part of a much broader threat to global democracy.

In May 2019, five months before the National Day celebrations, I went to prison for the second time. I spent seven weeks at Lai Chi Kok Correctional Institution for violating a court injunction during the Umbrella Movement. I tried to comfort my parents by downplaying the situation, telling them that I had picked up enough prison speak at Pik Uk to blend in with the inmates. I joked that my biggest regret was having to miss the opening night of *Avengers: Endgame*, the sequel to *Avengers: Infinity War* which I'd watched and re-watched several times.

Before heading to prison, a foreign reporter asked me for a soundbite about my second incarceration and China's crackdown on pro-democracy activists in general. I thought about my discussion with my parents and said, 'This isn't our end game. Our fight against the CCP is an infinity war.'

The infinity war that has ravaged Hong Kong for years, I am afraid, may be coming soon to a political theatre near you.

Canary in the Coal Mine: A Global Manifesto for Democracy

礦坑裏的金絲雀: 全球民主宣言

At the CECC hearing on Capitol Hill in September 2019 I issued a dire warning to the United States congressional committee: 'What's happening in Hong Kong matters to the world. The people of Hong Kong are standing at the forefront to confront China's authoritarian rule. If Hong Kong falls, the next may be the free world.'

Hong Kong is my birthplace and my beloved home. There is far more to this magical place than meets the eye. Beyond the soaring skyscrapers and glistening shopping malls, the semi-autonomous territory is the only place on Chinese soil where citizens dare stand up to those in power – because our very existence depends on it. For better or worse, the tidal waves of resistance in recent years have transformed the financial centre into a political stronghold. Notwithstanding Beijing's effort to keep the city in a state of perpetual adolescence, the latter has outgrown itself and its master. Hong Kongers, too, have evolved from detached economic beings to noble freedom fighters. Ever since the Handover we have been waging a lonely and improbable battle against an autocratic superpower with what little resources we have: our voice, our dignity and our conviction.

From Turkey and Ukraine to India, Myanmar and the Philippines, citizens are pushing back oppressive regimes in defence of their diminishing rights. But nowhere else in the world is the struggle between free will and authoritarianism more clearly demonstrated than here. In the new trans-Pacific cold war, Hong Kong is the first line of defence to stop or at least slow down the dangerous rise of a totalitarian superpower. Like the canary in the coal mine or the early warning system on a tsunami-prone coastline, we are sending out a distress signal to the rest of the world so that countermeasures can be taken before it is too late. As much as Hong Kong needs the international community, the international community needs Hong Kong. Because today's Hong Kong is the rest of the world's tomorrow.

The best way to illustrate this point is to understand the 'white terror' that has plagued Hong Kong since it reverted to Chinese rule. The term refers to the systematic attack on free expression and other democratic values, not through hard military might but by more subtle forms of fear and intimidation. For years, local businesses in Hong Kong have been pressured into keeping quiet on sensitive political subjects or openly siding with the Chinese government to avoid angering Beijing or alienating the lucrative mainland market. Media outlets in Hong Kong are known to self-censor for fear of losing advertising revenue. A-list celebrities have appeared in video confessionals to apologise for 'hurting the feelings' of the Chinese people after inadvertently wading into political debates. The feelings of the Chinese people are so easily and frequently hurt that a new phrase has been coined – we call it 'brittle heart syndrome'.

At the height of the anti-Extradition Bill protests, Cathay Pacific – Hong Kong's flagship airline that relies heavily on the Chinese market – fired two-dozen pilots and flight attendants who were sympathetic to the protesters. The airline's CEO issued a letter to all 33,000 staff warning them that they could be dismissed for making pro-protest social media posts and encouraging them to report 'unacceptable behaviour' among staff. The incident happened while I was in Washington DC, which prompted me to make a remark to House Speaker Nancy Pelosi after our press conference. 'This is a prime example of the white terror I mentioned in my testimony this morning,' I said. 'Let's hope what happened to Cathay Pacific will never happen to American companies.'

Less than a month after I said those fateful words, the National Basketball Association controversy exploded and set off one of the biggest PR crises in the history of professional sports. In October 2019, Daryl Morey, general manager of the Houston Rockets, posted a tweet in support of the Hong Kong protests. Morey's comment triggered a massive backlash in China resulting in cancelled events, pulled advertisements and a boycott by mainland basketball fans. When NBA Commissioner Adam Silver told reporters that Beijing had put pressure on the franchise to fire Morey, China's state broadcaster China Central Television (CCTV) warned Silver of 'retribution sooner or later' and 'dramatic financial consequences'.

Within the same month, US games publisher Blizzard Entertainment found itself in a similar diplomatic quagmire. Fearing backlash in China, Blizzard suspended e-sports gamer Ng Wai Chung for openly supporting the Hong Kong protesters and stripped him of his prize money (which was subsequently restored following international outcry). Then Apple bowed to pressure from Beijing and removed from its app store HKmap.live, a crowd-sourcing app that protesters had used to track police movements to evade arrest. In response to Apple's decision I wrote an open letter to CEO Tim Cook urging him to honour his commitment to free speech in the face of Chinese oppression. I did so not because I expected a response or change of heart from Apple, but because I wanted to send an urgent message to the international community. If even Apple – the world's leading tech giant and one that has in the past fought tooth and nail against the US authorities in defence of user privacy – finds itself bowing to authoritarian pressure, then how can we expect any other company or person to stand up to China in the future?

Even though these high-profile fallouts, all happening within a short space of time, have sent shockwaves around the world, they are 'old news' to us. The people of Hong Kong have grown so accustomed to this type of Orwellian state intimidation that it no longer shocks us. Sadly, what has been happening in Hong Kong for years is now happening to the rest of the world. Citizens everywhere are finally waking up to the reality that Communist China is increasingly throwing its weight around and mobilising its people to coerce foreign companies to comply with its worldview. That makes

China, simultaneously the most powerful autocratic regime and the largest consumer market on the planet, the single biggest threat to global democracy. The *New York Times* columnist Farhad Manjoo called the country 'a growing and existential threat to human freedom across the world'.

Our struggle has become your struggle, whether you like it or not. It is for this precise reason that the free world cannot stand idly by while the situation in Hong Kong continues to deteriorate. If Hong Kong fails, so goes the world's first line of defence. And if governments and multinationals continue to bend to the arc of China's gravity, it won't be long before citizens everywhere feel the same sting we have felt every day for the past two decades. In supporting Hong Kong in its resistance against the Communist regime, the international community is contributing to a broader fight against the spread of tyranny that, like climate change and terrorism, threatens the way of life and liberty everywhere. That's why to stand with Hong Kong is to stand with freedom. And that's why you must act now, before it's too late.

A perfect storm is brewing in the East. Xi's China is coming under increasing strain from the economic drag of an escalating trade war with the US on the one hand, and regional unrests in Xinjiang,

Tibet and Hong Kong on the other. Meanwhile, with a dangerous combination of rising unemployment and inflation, social discontent on the mainland is bubbling to the surface, the latter exacerbated by an epidemic of African swine fever that has driven up the price of pork, an important staple. Facing destabilising challenges on all sides, Xi is betting on strengthening his position by fomenting nationalism in China and stepping up his crackdown on dissent. He is hoping to navigate himself out of these turbulent times with a heavier hand and swifter measures, which in turn makes my call to stand with Hong Kong more urgent and critical than ever. The withdrawal of the Extradition Bill by the Hong Kong government is symbolically significant in that it is the first ever compromise made by Xi since he took power in 2012. Our hard-fought win suggests that the Mao-like strongman is not invincible and that there is light at the end of the tunnel if only we work together. Think about it: if a bunch of leaderless young people wearing basic protective gear can wring a concession from the world's most powerful autocratic regime with one of the world's biggest military forces, then imagine what we can achieve if all of us act together.

That is why I am asking for your help.

If my journey of activism has shown one thing, it is that even one person can make a difference no matter the odds. Whatever your age, wherever you are, you can be a part of something far greater than yourself. If you would like to help reverse the regression of democratic rights in Hong Kong and around the world, follow the ten-point action plan I set out below:

1. **Open a Twitter account** and follow hashtags such as #StandWithHongKong, #HongKong Protests and #FreedomHK. Translate tweets you find particularly relevant or inspiring into your own language so they can reach more people.

2. **Follow Hong Kong's news events** on independent news outlets like *Hong Kong Free Press* (www.hongkongfp.com) and, if you can read Chinese, *Stand News* (www.thestandnews.com).

3. **Participate in overseas Hong Kong protests** in your city. Create your own Lennon Walls (street murals of handwritten pro-democracy messages on sticky notes) or come up with an ice-bucket challenge-type viral campaign to promote awareness about the situation in Hong Kong and the threat to democratic rights posed by China and other autocratic regimes.

4.   **Watch the Hong Kong film** *Ten Years* **(2015),** the Ukrainian documentary *Winter on Fire: Ukraine's Fight for Freedom* (2015), and the Korean drama *1987: When the Day Comes* (2017). These movies will inspire you – as they have inspired me – to join the global fight against tyranny and social injustices.

5.   **Travel to Hong Kong** to get a first-hand look at the situation and speak to young Hong Kongers about their beliefs and experiences in the streets. Experience the city in all its glamour and trauma.

6.   **Write to your government officials** and legislators urging them to impose sanctions on Hong Kong government officials and the Hong Kong Police Force. Write a letter to the United Nations Security Council urging them to put pressure on China to guarantee freedom and democracy in Hong Kong. You can download templates from www.demosisto.hk.

7.   **Sign online petitions in support** of Hong Kong and anywhere else in the world where citizens' free expression or other fundamental rights are under threat.

8. **Support businesses and media outlets** that stand up to white terror from China or other autocratic regimes. Similarly, avoid companies that sacrifice free expression for short-term profit by yielding to oppressive governments. You can get a list of businesses we encourage you to support and those to avoid on www. demosisto.hk.

9. **Make a donation** to the Washington DC-based Hong Kong Democracy Council (www.hkdc.us/ donate), which has worked tirelessly over the years to lobby the US government to support the democratisation of Hong Kong.

10. **Tell five of your friends** about what you have learned from this book and share Hong Kong's story with them. Explain to them why standing with Hong Kong is standing with freedom and democracy.

One of the questions I am frequently asked when addressing student audiences overseas is how ordinary citizens can act on the erosion of democratic values in their own countries. As much as they sympathise with the situation in Hong Kong, they are equally if not more concerned about their declining freedoms at home. With the rise of far-right political parties in the West and a similar surge in populism elsewhere in the world, even advanced economies are not spared the same 'boiling frog' scenario facing Hong Kong. Below are five things you can do to counter this global threat:

1. **Follow news events** and identify warning signs where you live, such as increased political polarisation, citizen surveillance, paid advertisements by special interest groups and the use of police force on non-violent protests.

2. **Speak up about these warning signs** by sharing your thoughts on social media, talking to your local representatives and joining a civil society group that speaks to your concerns. Remember the slogan 'when you see something, say something'. Take a small step by attending one civil society event and see whether it makes you feel more empowered and energised. If not, try a different one.

3. **Learn to spot misinformation** in social media posts and news feeds. Visit fact-checking sites and discuss news events with friends, which I believe is the best way to develop media literacy

and hone your skills in telling apart real and fake news.

4. **Volunteer in the election campaign** of a political candidate to whom you relate. Few things will give you a better grasp of the democratic process than understanding the electoral system and immersing yourself in a campaign from start to finish.

5. **Organise your own small-scale rally** on issues that concern you – or in response to the warning signs you have identified in step 1. Work with like-minded friends to create simple banners and placards. Remember: every successful campaign starts with one voice, one flyer and one speech. Believe in the power of the individual.

There is a popular refrain in the restless streets of Hong Kong: 'This is our problem and we will solve it ourselves.' It is a show of courage, faith and self-reliance. But what if our problem is also yours? What if our problem is so vast that the only way to solve it is together?

Everything that I've done since I was 14 – Scholarism, Demosistō, national education, the Umbrella

Movement, from the principal's office to the prison cell, speaking at Civic Square and testifying on Capitol Hill – has led me to this point: Hong Kong's most desperate, but also its finest, moment. With your help and the help of the international community, Hong Kong will prevail and so will democracy across the globe, because this canary may be the best hope the world has to counter China's growing hegemony.

We are all in this together.

Epilogue

結語

In October 2019, two weeks after my testimony on Capitol Hill, the US House of Representatives passed the Hong Kong Human Rights and Democracy Act. A month later, the US Senate passed the Act before President Donald Trump signed it into law. Senator Marco Rubio, who had proposed the legislation, said on the Senate floor, 'The United States [has] sent a clear message to Hong Kongers fighting for their long-cherished freedoms: we hear you, we continue to stand with you, and we will not stand idly by as Beijing undermines your autonomy.'

In the meantime, US Senator Josh Hawley drafted the Hong Kong Be Water Act, calling for sanctions to combat the suppression of free expression by the Hong Kong and Chinese governments. The bill was proposed two days after local election authorities barred me from running in the District

Council on the grounds that Demosistō's self-determination platform is in breach of the Basic Law – the same reason they had banned Agnes from the LegCo election in 2018.

While sanctions against Hong Kong officials are a welcome development, they have done little to ease the tensions on our streets. As I am writing this, the city is still witnessing sporadic bursts of violence. In November 2019, for instance, riot police raided the Chinese University of Hong Kong and fired more than 1,500 rounds of tear gas and over 1,300 rubber bullets at demonstrators on a single day of confrontation. A week later, law enforcement besieged the Polytechnic University, trapping over a thousand protesters on campus for over 48 hours before most of them surrendered to the police.

Prolonged unrest has paralysed the city's traffic and public transport systems. Many restaurants, shops, banks and other businesses have been forced to shut. Tourism has plummeted and major international sporting and cultural events have been cancelled or postponed.

These incidents have created dramatic consequences for our city. Combined with the impact of an ongoing US–China trade war, Hong Kong officially slipped into recession late last year after the economy shrank for a second quarter in a row. While the government is quick to point fingers at the protesters, most of the blame falls on the Hong Kong Police who have been responding to demonstrations with disproportionate force and, in some cases, acts of retaliatory brutality.

The anti-Extradition Bill protests show no sign of abating. The movement has evolved into a rolling crisis that keeps Hong Kong society on a simmer. A stunning, landslide victory for the pro-democracy camp in the November 2019 District Council elections (which I was banned from running in) was widely seen as a referendum on the protest movement and led to a temporary 'ceasefire' between protesters and police.

But this truce is fragile. All it takes is another misstep by the government or riot police to trigger a resurgence in violence in a seemingly endless cycle of clashes, crackdowns and arrests. Nobody knows when, how and if the unrest will come to an end.

What we do know is the longer it goes on, the higher the price both sides will have to pay. Nearly 6,000 protesters, a substantial portion of whom are below the age of 18, have been arrested and charged with serious crimes such as rioting, arson and assault on police officers. There have been unconfirmed reports of fatalities being dressed up by the police as suicides. They say the night is darkest before dawn. In our case, the night is still young and our journey will get darker and more perilous before it gets better.

In the meantime, I continue to travel around the world to tell the story of Hong Kong and rally international support for our struggle. In-between my trips I set aside time for prison visits as there are a few dozen activists still behind bars and they need all the support we can give them. Considering how many young people have been arrested and charged in the still unravelling political unrest, hundreds more are expected to lose their freedom in the coming months.

Political imprisonment is an inevitable step on the path to democracy; it was the case in South Korea and Taiwan and it has been so in Hong Kong. Far from silencing us, prison will only strengthen our resolve. We have unfinished business and we won't stop until our demand for the most fundamental of all rights – a free vote and an accountable government – is met. From here on out, we'll stop asking nicely and start shouting so the rest of the world can hear us.

3 December 2019

Acknowledgements

致謝

———

It's by God's grace that the path of political activism has taken me this far and made me the person I am today. And so first and foremost I want to thank God for watching over me, my family, and the city I fight for.

None of what I do would have been possible – or had any meaning – if it weren't for my parents: my father who named me after the great prophet Joshua, raised me to be an honest man and taught me to be every bit as stubborn and persistent as he; my mother whose patience and care have helped me not only overcome my dyslexia but also become more compassionate and empathetic toward even those I have every reason not to be. It's said that when you become an activist, you bring your whole family with you. In the past ten years, I've put my parents through trying times, given them many sleepless nights, denied them precious family time and done pitifully little to make up for the sacrifices they've made. I'd like to give mum and dad my deepest apologies and sincerest thanks.

Then there's my other family: the young men and women of Demosistō. I'd like to thank my partner-in-crime, Ivan Lam, who has stuck with me through the rollercoaster ride from the early Scholarism days to every trial and tribulation that Demosistō has seen. Ivan never asks for any recognition but I want to give credit where credit's long overdue: he's hands-down the most trusted member in our team. I'm equally grateful to have Nathan Law fighting alongside me. Nathan's LegCo win remains the most beautiful battle I've fought in my political career. Thanks also go to Agnes Chow who has persevered through the ups and downs of Scholarism and Demosistō and under the often unforgiving glare of the media; Jeffrey Ngo whose efforts in international networking have taken Demosistō – and Hong Kong – to the world stage; Chris Kwok, friend and colleague since the anti-national education campaign; Lili Wong who listens to and comforts me always; Tobias Leung who works hard and plays hard; Arnold Chung who keeps me on my toes by challenging my views; Isaac Cheng, our youngest spokesperson; Tiffany Yuen, who taught me how to carry myself in public; Ian Chan who works tirelessly behind the scenes; Angus Wong and Kelvin Lam, both of whom have devoted themselves to district affairs; and Au Nok Hin, my mentor in community outreach. All of them have guided and tolerated me over the years and made my journey in activism less lonely and more colourful.

Thanks to lifelong friends and mentors Jacky Yu, Kerrie Wong and Justin Yim who have supported and inspired me since those halcyon days at UCC; Dorothy Wong who looks after her 'kids' in Demosistō, got us through some of the worst public relations crises, and is nothing short of a fairy god-mother to all of us; S.K. who helped me 'reintegrate' into civil society after my prison release and is the sister I never had; Tiffany C. who taught me an important lesson in life and will always have a place in my heart; and Fanny Y., Oscar L. and K.C., for being trusted friends and confidantes who dispense daily encouragement and counsel. Special thanks go to S.H. who visited me and looked after my affairs while I was behind bars, stood by me through my darkest and loneliest days, and has given me a reason to smile even in the most hopeless of situations.

I'd like to express my gratitude toward every local and foreign reporter who covers the pro-democracy movement in Hong Kong. Their professionalism, fearlessness and relentless pursuit of the truth are truly inspirational. Special thanks to journalists

Vivian Tam and Gwyneth Ho, both of whom have interviewed, profiled and guided me since day one. I also want to thank my legal team, in particular Jonathan Man, Donna Yau, Bond Ng, Jeffrey Tam and Lawrence Lok, who helped me through every grueling trial and court hearing and demonstrated by example the critical role played by human rights lawyers in a political movement.

My warmest thanks go to Martin Lee, the Father of Democracy in Hong Kong, who taught me everything I know in international lobbying and continues to coach me and educate me to this day; Anna Cheung, who supports us in New York and Washington D.C.; the indefatigable Eddie Chu, pro-democracy lawmaker who has given Demosistō his unconditional support; and filmmaker Matthew Torne, producer Andrew Duncan and director Joe Piscatella for believing in me and telling my story on film.

In regard to the book, I want to thank my co-author Jason Y. Ng who has supported me and my cause since our first interview at the Foreign Correspondents' Club years ago. He has brought this challenging project to fruition by lending his craft as a skilled nonfiction writer and coaxing long-forgotten dialogues and memories that I never thought would be relevant or noteworthy and that turned out to be the glue that holds the narrative together and the sparkle that brings my story to life. Jason's writing is matched by his culinary finesse. It's always a pleasure spending late nights at his place exchanging political views over his delicious home-cooked food.

I'd also like to thank my literary agent, Penguin Random House editor Hana Teraie-Wood and publisher Drummond Moir, all of whom are respected professionals in their fields who have guided me through the process and have been a genuine pleasure to work with. I'm indebted to the support that Penguin Random House has thrown behind this project despite the political climate and potential pressure they may face. This book, my first written for the international audience, would not have been possible without their interest and faith in Hong Kong.

Last but not least, I want to thank the courageous people of Hong Kong, as well as the generous support of people around the world for me and for my city.

Joshua Wong

I've devoted my career to writing about Hong Kong – my birthplace, my sole source of inspiration and in my mind the most splendid, captivating, fickle, paradoxical and frustrating place on the planet. Telling its stories is a life's work but also a tremendous privilege. Likewise, when I was approached to co-write Joshua's memoir, I felt both duty-bound to do justice to the man's meteoric rise from a teenage activist to an international human rights icon and honoured to be entrusted with that colossal responsibility. I'd like to thank Joshua for his confidence and faith in me and, above all, everything that he has done for our city. Hong Kong is lucky to have a fighter like him.

I'd like to thank all those who have helped me in my research, especially Joshua's family and his friends and colleagues at Demosistō. I'm also grateful to my partner Jack Chang for putting up with me during these reclusive months of writing; my agent for her patience and guidance; editor Hana Teraie-Wood and publisher Drummond Moir who are as insightful as they are delightful to work with; and Penguin Random House for standing behind this project, which requires courage and fortitude.

As this book goes to print, Hong Kong continues to be embroiled in a political crisis that's unprecedented in both scale and intensity. I'd like to thank every brave young woman and man out on the streets who are fighting for the future of our city with what little they have and everything they have.

Jason Y. Ng

Timeline of Key Events

大事表

———

1842	China cedes Hong Kong Island to Britain
1 October 1949	Mao Zedong founds the People's Republic of China
1958–1962	The Great Leap Forward in China
1966–1976	The Cultural Revolution in China
19 December 1984	Signing of the Joint Declaration by Britain and China over the return of Hong Kong
4 June 1989	Tiananmen Square Massacre in Beijing, China
1 July 1997	Handover of Hong Kong from Britain to China; Tung Chee-hwa becomes first chief executive of Hong Kong
1997–1998	Asian Financial Crisis

11 December 2001	China joins World Trade Organization
2003	SARS outbreak in Hong Kong
25 June 2005	Donald Tsang becomes second chief executive of Hong Kong
2011	China becomes the world's second largest economy
29 May 2011	Joshua Wong founds student activist group Scholarism
1 July 2012	C.Y. Leung becomes third chief executive of Hong Kong
8 October 2012	C.Y. Leung announces the withdrawal of the national education curriculum after Scholarism leads hundreds of thousands in a mass sit-in
15 November 2012	Xi Jinping becomes president and paramount leader of the People's Republic of China
31 August 2014	China's National People's Congress Standing Committee issues '31 August framework' restricting the free election of Hong Kong's chief executive
26 September 2014	Storming of Civic Square by members of Scholarism over restrictive electoral reform

28 September 2014	Tear gas crackdown by riot police on peaceful pro-democracy protesters; start of Umbrella Movement
15 December 2014	Umbrella Movement ends
8 February 2016	Mongkok Chinese New Year civil unrest
10 April 2016	Joshua Wong and Nathan Law co-found political party Demosistō
21 July 2016	Conviction of Joshua Wong, Nathan Law and Alex Chow for unlawful assembly and incitement over storming of Civic Square in 2014
4 September 2016	Nathan Law becomes youngest ever lawmaker in Hong Kong
1 July 2017	Carrie Lam becomes fourth chief executive of Hong Kong
14 July 2017	Nathan Law loses his LegCo seat for straying from prescribed oath during swearing-in ceremony (Oathgate)
Aug	shua Wong, lex Chow bly and

13 October 2017	Conviction of Joshua Wong, Lester Shum and several other protesters of contempt of court
9 April 2019	Conviction of Occupy Central Trio and several other activists for their roles in Umbrella Movement
16 May 2019	Second incarceration of Joshua Wong for contempt of court
9 June 2019	Start of anti-Extradition Bill political crisis
16 June 2019	2 million Hong Kong citizens take to the streets demanding complete withdrawal of the Extradition Bill
5 September 2019	Carrie Lam announces withdrawal of the Extradition Bill
24 November 2019	District Council elections see landslide victory for pro-democracy camps
28 November 2019	US enacts Hong Kong Human Rights and Democracy Act